The Snowball
Leveraging Real Estate to Reach Financial Freedom

Art Agirian

Copyright © 2021 Art Agirian
All rights reserved.
ISBN: 9798760573575

DEDICATION

This book is dedicated to everyone who currently thinks financial freedom is not possible given their current circumstances. This book will provide the kick in the ass you need to get started. No matter your education level, or current financial situation, anyone who makes the decision to achieve financial freedom can do so through real estate

Table of Contents

Preface 3

Cool Kid Syndrome 7

My First Investment 11

The Snowball Effect 19

Cash-Out Refinance – Do vs. Don't 26

What if the Economy Crashes? 33

Leveraging Technology to Build Your Team 39

Flipping vs. Buy and Hold 49

Math > Love 57

Out of State vs. Local Investing 63

Opportunities in Any Market 71

Passive Income > Earned Income 75

Uncle Sam 80

Run It Like a Business, Man. 88

Anti-401K 92

Budgeting 101 97

Appreciate the Appreciation 104

DTI 109

Inspection Period Is Your Best Friend 114

Pre-Approval 120

Property Classes 124

Tenant Screening 128

Summary 134

ACKNOWLEDGMENTS

To anyone who has contributed to my journey, thank you. The ride is nowhere near complete and we have many more milestones to reach, but I couldn't be where I am now without the support of the people closest to me.

Preface

I want you to take a second and think about why you picked up this book... Was it because you're sick of working for someone else in your 9-5 job? Was it because you've came to the realization that you have to work 5 days a week till you are 65+ years old to finally retire and supposedly start enjoying your life? How are you supposed to enjoy your life when you're 65 years old? Some people don't even live till they are 65 years old. Or maybe you're someone who's making tens of thousands every month but have absolutely no financial plan in place? Was it because you realized you're tired of trading your time for money and having it not allow you to spend time with your loved ones and see your kids grow up?

I can probably list many many more reasons, but you get the point. And frankly, this is the reason why I decided to write this book to begin with. Most of the people in my life seem okay with the idea of working till they are old and gray to finally call it quits from the rat race with absolutely no financial planning in place. They just assume everything is going to be okay. This ideology gets under my skin. I get agitated with friends, family members all the time and at times I feel like I'm the dumb one for being the outsider.

That's when I take a couple deep breaths and think about all the cash flow I'm going to be making while sitting on my couch drinking tea without any worries in the world while everyone else is still slaving away. Or just maybe I might be able to convince them of otherwise.

I want to be able to share my Real Estate journey with the world and if it even helps just one single person out there, I would be satisfied. Don't get me wrong, I am nowhere near where I want to be in life, but over the last 8 years I can confidently say I've made drastic strides towards financial independence. As I'm writing this book, I can actually say my cash flow from the properties I own has surpassed the net income I make from my 9-5. What does that mean? I can quit right now and still live my normal everyday life and I'd be okay. That type of certainty changes a person. It changes your whole mindset. It's not only made me more confident in the Real Estate world but believe it or not it's made me more confident in my 9-5 job even though they are not directly connected in any way. Why is that the case? Let me explain. The second my rental property income surpassed by W2 income, I was no longer working because I had to. I was working because I *wanted* to. That's probably one of the most powerful statements you'll read in this book so highlight it, circle it, do whatever you have to do to remember it.

Now that doesn't mean I'm going to march into work and give my notice – Having this job is what's helped me get to where I am. I'm sure you've heard the saying that goes something like banks love lending to someone with a W2 job. Having the steady income has helped me qualify for the loans I have today so I'm thankful. One day I will decide to call it quits but not yet!

As you continue reading along, I think it's important for me to mention I've had no special outside advantages in my journey – I grew up an average human being. I was not given a trust fund of any sorts. I started working a minimum wage retail job at a golf shop right out of high school. I knew absolutely nothing about golf. The only reason I applied there was because one of my high school friends was working there at the time and I needed a job. I was pretty much selling golf clubs to rich white men and giving them advice on which clubs would help make them become better golfers – Again, I had absolutely no knowledge about golf and I was completely bullshitting out of my ass. I wonder how many rich white men out there golfing are using the completely wrong golf clubs because of me. I'm telling you this only so you understand I did not have any special advantageous. I did have a family that cared, put a roof over my head and had food on the table and I'm thankful for that. In today's world some would call this privileged and to some extent it probably was. But again, I did not have any special financial head start. I'm also not some multi-millionaire trying to sell you on some get rich quick scheme. I am not even a multi-millionaire. My net worth from the properties I own just recently surpassed one million and that was a big accomplishment for me. I'm telling you all this because I want you to know that an average human being with no financial head start in life can accomplish financial freedom through Real Estate and not be forced to work for a paycheck 5 days a week till they are 65 years old. Everyone's number one goal in their financial planning should be *not* to trade time for money and the way to do this is by increasing your passive income, not your earned income.

With all that being said, I entered my twenties and no matter what I decided to do in life moving forward, I knew I needed to make it on my own.

And so here is my journey...

Chapter 1

Cool Kid Syndrome

"Ninety percent of all millionaires become so through owning real estate."

Andrew Carnegie

I was twenty-one years old living under my mother's roof paying no rent and working at this golf shop. I would go out every weekend with my group of friends to wherever the cool kids were hanging out that day. I felt special. I was able to take my entire paycheck and spend it on all the food, alcohol, club entrance fees, and whatever other stupid thing came up on any given adventurous night out. I was working five days a week to pay for my Friday and Saturday nights. But I was missing something... I didn't have a nice expensive car like some of the friends I was hanging with. That might have meant I wasn't as cool or the girls we were hanging out with might not like me as much as everyone else. So, what did I do? You guessed it! I went out and financed a brand-new Mercedes e350 coupe with a payment of $900 a month using all the money I had saved from birthdays, holidays, etc. for the down payment. In case you forgot let me remind you, I was working in a golf shop making minimum wage. This my friends is the definition of what 99% of people do their entire life. They will sacrifice everything for that instant gratification because to them looking cool and having nice things right now is all that matters even if it means sacrificing their future and I was no exception at the time.

To make matters even worse, I was already a disappointment to my family from the start because I went to a junior college for half a semester and dropped out – Why did I drop out? Because I got promoted to a full-time position at the golf shop. I still replay moments in my head till this day of family members asking me what my plans were and what I was doing for employment and their faces when I told them I was working in retail at this golf shop. I cringe remembering the facial expressions everyone would make.

This absurd $900 a month car payment fiasco lasted a little over a year. I'm not sure what changed – maybe it was one drunken night where I questioned what I was doing with my life. Or maybe it was because I was counting the scraps left in my pocket for food and drinks after making that $900 payment on the 1st of every month. Needless to say, one day I woke up and came to my damn senses. I drove the Mercedes coupe straight to CarMax and asked to get my vehicle appraised to see how much I could possibly sell it for and officially get it off my hands. I had done zero research and had no idea what they were going to come back with. Frankly, I thought I might be upside down on the loan and would have to donate more money to this horrible life decision I had made. The CarMax employee slowly approached with the piece of paper in his hands that had what they were willing to offer me for the vehicle. This was such a nerve wrecking moment, and his 20 feet walk seemed like it took about 20 minutes. The gentlemen handed me the piece of paper and when I saw the offer, I almost jumped into the guy's lap from excitement. They were offering 10K MORE than what I owed on the loan. For a second I thought I was being pranked. Is this really happening? Am I really about to walk out of here with a ten-thousand-dollar check? I sure as hell was and believe me, I never looked back! This is not a CarMax sponsorship, but hey if you have a car to sell I'd give it a whirl and try your luck.

Shortly after this I also moved on from the golf shop to another retailer who was offering me better pay and a better position. I was now making $15 an hour and in my mind this was a big step up. I was now removed from my $900 a month car payment and making a few bucks more an hour at a new company. I was headed in the right direction with a better mindset and the cool kid syndrome was finally coming to an end. Receiving that check for the Mercedes was almost like the universe giving me a second chance to make better decisions with my money. I had to get my shit together.

Chapter Summary:
- Don't sacrifice your future for the present by spending your money on shiny materialistic stuff. No one cares, and if they do care, they are probably not the people you should have within your inner circle.

Chapter 2

My First Investment

"The purpose of a budget is to help thy purse to fatten"

George S. Clason

I've always been attracted to money. As a young kid I remember I had twenty single dollar bills and my parents needed them – They offered to give me a single $20 bill in exchange for the twenty $1 bills that I had saved as a young kid. I refused this trade emphatically because in my own head I was getting ripped off. Why would I exchange twenty bills for just one?? This might not be the best example of someone who is money smart, but I tell you this short story to illustrate that even from a young age I've always been drawn to money and saw the value in it.

One quiet day I was home counting my money and budgeting to see how much I would be saving from the new job. I started weighing that vs. life expenses. See when you're young and have no responsibilities you don't really care about these things, and we all know the high school you went to definitely didn't teach you any of this crap either. After high school most kids plan to attend college where they STILL don't care about any of this stuff. Having skipped ahead in life responsibilities by not attending college I feel like I jumped a couple years ahead and started paying attention to the importance of my financial situation earlier than most usually would. What I quickly realized was that making $15 an hour was dog crap unless I planned on living under my mother's roof my whole life. It took me 3 years to get this new job – How was I going to survive and make it in life by getting a couple dollars more an hour every few years? There had to be another way – Many days I questioned whether my life choice of not going to school was about to come back and bite me from behind. The last thing I wanted to hear was everyone telling me "I told you so" with their upside-down facial expressions. And the fact is I know there are thousands if not millions of people out there who are currently in this exact same situation right now.

So if I wasn't willing to go back to school just to appease everyone around me, and I also didn't see a fast-track way to drastically accelerate my hourly wage, I needed another income stream. My next big life decision would carry a lot of force and horsepower behind it which would have ripple effects for years to come – This is described incredibly well by MJ DeMarco in his book "The Millionaire Fastlane."

We had a close family member who was a Real Estate agent and my mother worked in the property management field so naturally during a few family gatherings the housing market had come up in discussion. I didn't know much about Real Estate at the time, but I knew it was how rich people made a lot of money. That's how some of these rich men were able to visit the golf shop I worked in at 11am in the morning on a Wednesday to buy some golf balls. The year was 2012 and the economy was fresh off the housing market crash so home prices relatively speaking were affordable even though the financing was still tough. One day after spending some time on the internet browsing the listings on the MLS, I decided I wanted to take the money I had received from selling the car and use it to purchase a piece of property. I reached out to our family friend Real Estate agent Lily and explained to her what I had planned and she agreed to help me out.

And the slow painful grind you feel when starting something new had officially started. I was living in California at the time and even though prices were more reasonable during 2012, there's still only a handful of places you're able to really afford with $10,000 of buying power. Nowadays you see so many people preaching about how you can buy Real Estate with no money down. Is it possible? Yes. Is it common? No. I'm not going to be one of these people who say you can get started with no money. Truth is most people need some sort of down payment to get their foot through the door. Networking with individuals who would be willing to trust their hard-earned money to someone brand new with no experience is not likely to happen unless you have a close family member that's willing to help you out. The only other option you would have is to use a hard money lender and pay 8-10% interest. Not for me thank you very much. Also, keep in mind we're only talking about buy and hold Real Estate here. Sure, if you're trying to flip homes the chances of utilizing a hard money lender to get started would be doable, but this is not the case when you're strictly doing buy and hold transactions.

Months went by and we weren't able to find anything on the open market. Most would have probably quit or given up already, but I had committed and wasn't going to let anything stop me from taking my first step in this journey.

As listing after listing was going by, we came across this condo not too far from where I was living. It was priced in the right ballpark at $135,000. I was a first-time home buyer and we were going to be using an FHA loan requiring just 3.5% down + closing costs. The property had been sitting on the market for over 30 days with no offers so we knew there was a chance we could get an offer accepted below asking. We decided to move forward and wrote the offer up at $120,000 and kept our fingers crossed. Alongside the offer we also wrote a letter around this being my first home purchase which added a nice sentimental touch. The waiting period to hear back on an offer is horrible. It's like texting a girl you really like and waiting for the response, constantly looking at your phone every 2 minutes to see if they've responded. A couple days went by and I got the call from my agent Lily – They had accepted our offer! I thought it was time to celebrate, pop the champagne, que the music. What I didn't yet know is how excruciating of a process it is to get through the entire loan process with the lender. Be prepared to fork over every document you have ever received in your entire life. (I'm exaggerating of course) Here is a list of some of the most common documents you should be saving together in one place if you are planning on purchasing a home in the future.

- Two years of tax returns
- Anywhere from 2-12 months of bank statements
- Two years of your W2
- Statements of any other thing you have financed – Like your vehicle
- Credit card statements
- 401k statements
- Paystubs
- Employment verification form

Now if you're a well-organized adult this might seem easy for you. When you're a 22-year-old kid not so easy. In most of these examples above it was my very first time even trying to locate these documents. Additionally, any money you plan on using to pay for the home should be saved in your personal bank account and be within the "seasoning" period. Most lenders do not want to see big deposits into your account within the previous two months before the purchase of the home, otherwise it's going to raise major red flags on where the money came from. So if you need to move money around to your main account in order to pay for the down payment, make sure you do all that months ahead of time so you don't run into any issues. To sum up here the loan process is a pain in the ass and to save yourself at least some of the headache you need to have your paperwork ready to go.

Finally, around 45 days later we officially closed on the loan. My mortgage for the property was around $600 a month including property taxes and insurance. Since it was a condo there was also an association fee of around $200 a month. All-in my monthly expenses + principal was just about $800. Since my mom worked in the property management industry, we knew based on our research the unit should rent for about $1300-$1400 a month. That would give me a monthly cash flow of around $500 extra a month in addition to what I was making at my W2 job. At this time I had no idea what cash on cash return meant, or what the word cash flow meant. I just knew an extra $500 a month meant I was winning in life and if I could repeat this multiple times I wouldn't need to work anymore. ANYONE can do this. Please be aware though, when you purchase a home as your primary residence, most lenders will require you to live in the property for at least a year. Unforeseen circumstances and/or major life changes can obviously come into play so make sure you're not doing anything that's going to get you in trouble. We will also talk a little more about house hacking later on in the book which is a strategy that can be utilized to slowly grow your portfolio even if you're making a purchase as a primary residence. I was 22 years old. Knew nothing about Real Estate. I just made the decision to go for it and at the time I didn't even realize how big of an impact this was going to have on my future.

This small, tiny investment 8 years ago catapulted my Real Estate career and transformed how I viewed my life expectations. This small investment made me believe I didn't need to work my whole life to retire at 65 years old. It made me believe I didn't need a college degree from a university that would have costed me 6 figures. It made me believe financial independence was achievable even for someone starting from nearly zero.

Chapter Summary:
- One small real estate investment can change the trajectory of your entire financial future.
- Real estate makes financial freedom possible for anyone willing to jump in.

Chapter 3

The Snowball Effect

"It's not how much money you make, but how much money you keep, how hard it works for you, and how many generations you keep it for."

Robert Kiyosaki

Imagine standing in the middle of a quiet road on a bright sunny day with the temperature a perfect 75 degrees. The birds are chirping, the light breeze is gently blowing, and everything is perfect. Then BOOM. A snowball of money hits you right in the face. Welcome to the snowball effect of Real Estate. This is when you realize you've almost made it to the finish line of reaching financial freedom.

When I bought my first condo as a young kid in his early twenties, I really didn't understand the magnitude of what that decision would lead to in the future at the time. I was living in the moment and all I could see was the potential to making an extra $500 a month in rental income.

During those 18 months the Real Estate market was on the up and up and home values were appreciating across the board. The condo I purchased was now worth $185,000. That is 65k more than what I originally purchased it for. You see aside from the fear of losing money, the second reason most people do not invest in Real Estate is because they don't get that instant gratification from it. Real Estate is not a get rich quick game so for most people the thought process in their head is something like... "I'm supposed to put all the hard-earned money in my savings account towards a property and only make a few hundred dollars every month? No thank you I rather hold on to it." They do not see the big picture, and they do not have the patience to play this game. It's the exact same discipline required when you are trying to get fit by going to the gym. Someone with that same mindset would say... "I'm supposed to go to the gym 4-5 times a week and I'm not going to see any serious results for 4-6 months? No thank you. I rather stuff my face and get my instant gratification now." This type of thinking has become more and more like the norm because of social media. Especially in today's world, when everything you see on Instagram is about how someone got rich by investing in doge coin or bitcoin or some other stupid coin someone in their forties living at home with their mom created while sitting on the kitchen counter. Everyone wants the nice toys and they want it now. The sad truth is majority of people who are chasing this instant gratification are not going to make it and they're going to end up struggling trying to make ends meet for their entire life.

If you have the patience, the discipline, and if you want to ensure you reach financial freedom you need to invest in Real Estate.

In 18 months', my net worth grew by 65K just on this one small rental property. During this time, I learned what a cash-out refinance was. You mean I get to take out equity from my property and not pay any taxes on the cash? Sign me up. Here's a quick tutorial on a cash-out refinance. My new home value was appraised at 185k. At the time I currently owed around 110k to the bank – If you remember I purchased the condo for 120k but minus the down payment and the payments over the 18 months my loan had gone down to around the 110k mark. With a cash-out refinance you can get a new loan for 80% of the appraised value. It's almost like pretending you're about to re-purchase the same home for the new appraised value because that's actually what it's worth and you're going to put 20% down. So 185k minus 20% down which would be 37K. That would make the new loan amount 148K. But here's the best part – I only owed 110k on the loan that I had. This meant that the bank would give me a check for whatever that value in between was, so 148k minus 110k. If you have a brain or a smartphone with a calculator, you'd see that I would be getting a nice fat check of around 38 thousand dollars in my savings account. What did I do to deserve this money you ask? I sat on my couch watching Netflix and allowing Real

Estate to do what it does. Do you have the patience to play game? Or are you someone who just wants instant gratification right now and is willing to jeopardize their future for it.

I was 38K richer and to be honest I had never seen that much money in my savings account before. Most people would have gone out and splurged spending thousands of dollars at the mall or on some fancy new materialistic item... but not me. I was hooked. This is the moment I realized this game is not meant for everyone, but if you're willing to play and have the discipline to see it through, it's going to set you up not only for your life, but for generations and generations down the line. I want the grand-kids of my grand-kids to be living off the Real Estate empire that I decided to start – I want them to be sitting around the coffee table 100 years from now talking about how their great great grandfather decided to buy a condo for 120k when he was 22 years old with hardly any money and turned it into a damn money machine. You can plan on doing this for your family starting today. Right now.

So what did I decide to do with the 38k check I just received? That's right, I decided to go back out into this so-called scary world of Real Estate and purchase my second property!

I originally planned on taking you through the numbers for most of the transactions I've done, but I decided not to put you to sleep with more math problems. The only thing you really need to know is that I followed this same blueprint over the course of the next 4-5 years. I did get incremental raises at my W2 job over the course of those years, but the hard truth is that most of the money I've spent on Real Estate purchases have come from the properties themselves. They have funded each other with little dependency on what I was making at my 9-5. It only takes one small property to get the snowball rolling. It might start small, and you might barely feel the value of it in the moment, but as long as that snowball keeps rolling it's going to turn into the biggest rolling money machine you never even thought was possible. The one and only rule you need to follow is to not touch the cash flow money coming in. You need to be disciplined and have your eyes on the bigger picture. For this reason, I recommend opening another account where the rental income will go. Make sure this account is at a totally different bank than the one you're currently using so you are less likely to be tempted to just transfer it over to your personal account. By doing this, you're also allowing yourself to have a cleaner picture of your finances because every little personal expense will not get mixed into the rental income you're collecting.

I refinanced and took money out on my first 3 purchases, and with the third cash-out refinance I was able to fund my 4th property. This is when I realized the snowball was picking up some speed and growing at a high pace. I say this because with the 4th purchase, I was bringing home around $3,500 a month in positive cash flow. Over a course of a year that's an extra $42,000 in my pocket. This is important because I knew at this point I could easily re-invest my cash flow into new properties without even being dependent on doing another cash-out refinance. When you become a more experienced investor, you realize as great as a cash-out refinance is, at the end of the day you are starting a new loan with more debt, so if you're able to start funding new purchases without doing a cash-out refinance, you're going to start growing your net worth incrementally more every month while also being able to add more properties to your portfolio. It becomes a win win and your money starts growing at lightning speed.

Chapter Summary:
- Generational wealth. Real estate will remain in your family for generations, allowing all that come after you to reap the benefits of something you started.
- You will not have to save up years of income for every purchase. Through market forces, your properties will start to fund your next purchase.
- It only takes one small property to get the snowball rolling. It might start small, and you might barely feel the value of it in the moment, but as long as that snowball keeps rolling it's going to turn into the biggest rolling money machine you never even thought was possible

Chapter 4

Cash-Out Refinance – Do vs. Don't

"The best time to buy a home is always five years ago."

Ray Brown

We briefly touched on what a cash-out refinance is in the previous chapter, but I'd like to spend some time going over this topic in a little more detail because it is such a strong tool a Real Estate investor has in their toolbox. However, I want to discuss both sides of the coin. When most people hear about a cash-out refinance they seem to only talk about the perks and the good stuff, but never what the potential downside could be.

Let's start with the good first...

In my opinion, a cash-out refinance is the #1 tool to help a new investor scale their portfolio. Most people who have equity in their home feel safe and secure, but who cares about the equity in your home if you're not using it to grow! Over the course of the last 7-8 years, I've used and repeated the same process to help scale my portfolio to where it is now and the best part is I've used hardly any of my own money. I've leveraged the Real Estate I've purchased over and over again to add more properties and increase my monthly cash flow. The funny part is most people who are not investors will look at buying more property as a risk because you're taking on more debt when in reality the more cash flowing properties you're able to add to the portfolio the safer and less risky it is. If you have one home and you have an issue with a tenant, you're going to be stuck paying for that mortgage out of your own pocket but when you have a whole collection of properties chances are you will be able to afford that hit you're taking from that one rental. I can tell you the chances of having an issue with just one rental is a lot higher than having an issue with 10 rentals at once.

Utilizing the equity in your rentals also gives you flexibility for more than just Real Estate. Most middle-class families don't have 200K sitting in their savings account waiting for a rainy day, but guess what? If you buy Real Estate, I bet you in just a few years you'll have 200 thousand in equity if not more. So if you ever need an emergency fund for any of life's unexpected moments you don't have to go begging people for money because you'll have it on your own in your own property's equity.

Another great reason to utilize a cash-out refinance when you want to take advantage of your property's equity is you don't pay any taxes on the money you take out! If you sold the property you would be subject to a capital gains tax which can be up to 40% off the top. That's a huge amount to give to Uncle Sam. Wouldn't it be better to do a cash-out refinance for up to 80% of the appraised value and not pay ANY taxes on it? Hell yes it would. Now I'm not a tax accountant and this could have an impact down the line if you ever decide to sell your property so please discuss further with your CPA before taking action.

So the top three benefits for utilizing a cash-out finance are 1. Help scale your portfolio 2. Flexibility and access to large sums of cash for unexpected life circumstances and 3. Pay no taxes.

Now let's talk a little about the not so good stuff...

There's only one but it could come with big consequences if you're not careful and make you regret playing this Real Estate game. Over-leverage, over-leverage, over-leverage. I cannot stress this enough. Right now, as I'm writing this book is a great example of when people need to be careful. We have been in a strong seller's market for over 12 months where supply has been low, demand has been and continues to be high, and prices have been appreciating like gangbusters. I saw an Instagram post the other day that showed the average home-owner equity right now is around 250K. Even though banks are trying to get ahead of a potential issue and making it a bit tougher to do a cash-out refinance or open a HELOC, there are still plenty of banks out there that are doing so.

I have 2 rules that I need to check off before I decide to do a cash-out refinance or open a HELOC on a rental property. Rule #1 – I still need to be making a decent amount of cash flow from the property. When you decide to use your property's equity, your mortgage payment goes up because you're taking on more debt. If after doing the math you notice that the debt + expenses are going to be more than what you are receiving in rental income you should absolutely not go through with it. This goes for buying a property too. Do not take a property that is performing well for you and giving you monthly cash flow and turn it into a property that you have to pay out of your pocket every month just to get all the bills paid. This is how people lose everything and spread lies about how risky Real Estate is. Real Estate is not risky. You are just a dumbass who doesn't know how to properly run the numbers and YOU made the investment risky and therefore deserved the end result. You cannot tell yourself it's okay to have a rental property that isn't making you monthly income because it's going to go up in value over time and you will end up profiting from the appreciation. Could that be the case? Yes of course. But you are adding additional risk that you should not be taking, and you're losing money every month in the meantime. Rule #2 – The money cannot be planned to be used for anything else other than re-investing into another property. Obviously there could be emergency cases where you need to spend, but what I'm referring to is taking the money and purchasing a car or a boat or some other expensive materialistic items. When you're well off, yes you can 100% do this. But when you are still in the growing phase you cannot afford to do this because it will stunt your growth and set you back for years.

If used properly with a strong strategic plan in place, a cash-out refinance will help turn that snowball into an avalanche in just a few short years. You just need to be patient and disciplined. The money is going to come and it's going to make you filthy rich. The only question you need to ask yourself is are you up for it?

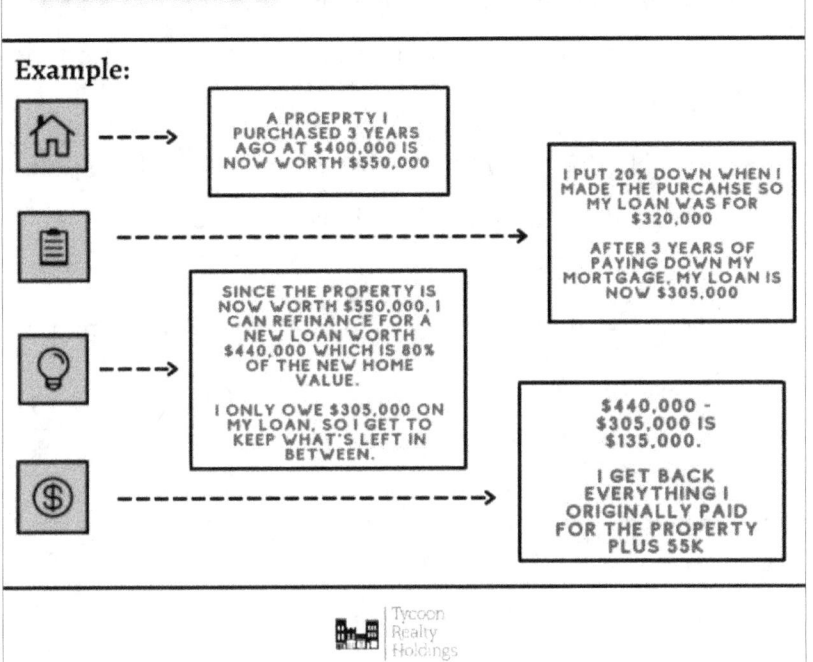

Chapter Summary:
- A cash-out refinance is the best tool an investor has to grow their real estate portfolio.
- You need to know the pros and cons of taking on more debt.
- Do NOT take your hard-earned property equity to purchase materialistic things or else it will set you back for years.
- Never end up with a mortgage that is more than your collected rent.

Chapter 5

What if the Economy Crashes?

"Landlords grow rich in their sleep."

John Stuart Mill

I love this question. Right when you hear someone say something about the Real Estate market crashing you automatically know they are full of shit and full of excuses. I'm sorry if that hurt's your feelings but it's true. It's always the same excuses no matter what the state of the market is – These individuals have never bought a property and chances are they never will. Here are a few examples of what these common statements will sound like...

"The Real Estate market is so expensive right now; we're going to wait till there is a crash before we decide to buy something"

"Omg why are you buying property, aren't you scared the market is going to crash."

"The market just crashed... It feels too dangerous to invest right now, we're going to keep our money in our savings just in case we need it."

"We can't afford a property right now; everything is too expensive." (As they get a brand-new car and pay $500 a month.")

Don't be this person. All you sound like when saying these things is simply that this isn't a priority for you. And if that's what you want that's okay. But don't lie to yourself and give out all these lame excuses about why you haven't bought an investment property yet. Step up. If you truly care stop with the bullshit. Come up with a plan and execute. Ask questions – I've learned 75% of what I know from googling stuff. There are free educational materials everywhere.

There are 3 core reasons why you should not care at all if the market crashes. Listen, no one should want or be waiting for the market to crash so the fact that people say things like that is ridiculous. When a market crashes home prices aren't the only thing that gets impacted. There is a list of other economic factors that would impact millions of people and no one should be asking for it. So back to my 3 core reasons...

First, this is why it is so critical to buy correctly going into it. There is a saying that goes something like "you make your money when you buy the property, not when you sell it "and this is exactly what I'm talking about. We will cover this in a lot more details in the chapter Math > Love but for now you can't just buy something because it looks cool and/or because you really like it. This is not an emotional game; you can save that for your life partner. When I buy a property, I make sure the monthly cash flow meets my criteria. As long as I stick to my plan, I know that even IF the market crashes, it will be impacting the amount of the home value not the amount of the rents I'm collecting every month. People are still going to need to rent a place to live. During a market crash people who own their own property are the ones that would be impacted the most. This is where being a long term buy and hold investor is a big plus. If I'm buying and holding for the long-term, I have the ability to wait out any market impact to the downside until it is able to recover even if that recovery takes years.

Secondly, if there is a market crash and people lose their homes, guess what? They're going to need a place to rent. In this scenario the rental demand actually increases and the overall property ownership percentage drops. I'm not an economic expert, but if you end up with higher demand with more people needing rentals, that is typically a good thing for the rental market so your properties would not be impacted at the same level.

Last but not least, interest rates and money printing. Typically, when there is some sort of market crash to the downside, interest rates get lowered to help boost the economy and more money gets printed to stimulate the economy. This is not specific to the housing market. The covid-19 shutdowns in 2020 is a great example of this. The economy went into a recession and overall interest rates went down to the lowest levels in history and the government planned on keeping them low till the economy was back to full strength and the job market was in a better place. They also printed more money in one year than ever before in history. To give you a real-life example from my own personal experience during this time, I had purchased a property in 2018 with an interest rate of 5.3%. With all my expenses and my mortgage, I was paying around $3,300 a month and my rental income was around $4,100 leaving me with $800 in cash flow. This was a great deal going in and I was extremely thrilled with the profit I was making every month. Well, fast-forward a couple years and a handful of months and we were right in the middle of all the covid-19 madness. However, with all the madness came lower interest rates to help pull the economy back on its feet. I decided to refinance this property and I was able to lower the original 5.3% and get myself locked into a new 30-year fix at just a 3.0% interest rate! By doing this I was able to lower the original $3,300 a month I was paying down to just $2,650. My rental income did not change so my new profit was now $1,450 every single month from this one property. That's how big of an impact the interest rate can have on your investment. I was able to increase my monthly cash flow by over $600 by just moving down the rate. Also, with all the money that's being printed and the home prices skyrocketing due to inflationary reasons, that 500K home from just a couple years ago was now valued at around 800K. The power of real estate...

As great of a win as this was for my overall portfolio, I want to make sure I highlight the fact that this was obviously not why I purchased the property. I didn't purchase the property on the hope that the property was going to appreciate, and I sure as hell didn't buy the property thinking that interest rates would continue to go down as much as they did. I bought the property because the math made since from the very beginning. Everything else that has happened since then has been icing on the cake and this is the type of mindset and discipline you need when purchasing an investment property.

If you've done the proper research and you've made this a priority, the state of the market will not matter to you. You will not sit there coming up with a bunch of excuses on why you are not buying a rental property, because if you had all of the correct information, you'd know that if the right deal came along nothing else matters. So from now on when you hear anyone say anything around market crashes and give you excuses on why they are not trying to buy a rental property, I want you to look them dead in the face and say... "Who the hell cares? Have you read The Snowball by Art Agirian?" and when they say no, hand them the book and end the conversation because that person is never going to change their mind period.

> **Chapter Summary:**
> - Take action and don't make stupid excuses.
> - Real estate is no different than anything else you decide to do in your life. If financial freedom is a priority for you, you will get it done just like you would hit the gym if getting in shape was a priority.

Chapter 6

Leveraging Technology to Build Your Team

"Money makes money, And the money that makes money makes more money."

Benjamin Franklin

Are you lazy? There's an app for that. Worried about not knowing what to do when a tenant has a clogged toilet? Don't worry, there's an app for that. Not sure how you would find a new tenant when someone leaves without proper notice? There's an app for that also.

We live in a time where we have access to everything we could possibly want and then some. I honestly don't think I would have been able to be successful at this whole Real Estate thing if I grew up in the 80's. I am not the most social butterfly in the world and I am not a great networker. Most days I would say this is my biggest opportunity personally, but we can probably save that for another book. As far as Real Estate goes, you can do absolutely everything you need to do from end to end utilizing either a computer or your mobile phone so there are absolutely zero excuses out there. I'm going to list my most used apps on my phone from the time I'm looking to make a new purchase all the way through to managing a tenant's lease!

1. Redfin
2. Zillow
3. Zillow – Rental Manager
4. Zillow – 3D Home
5. Hot Pads
6. Facebook Marketplace
7. QuickBooks
8. Thumbtack
9. Tiny Scanner
10. Credit Karma
11. Home Depot
12. Chase

Twelve apps in total are all you need to build everything you can possibly need for your Real Estate business. Let's now go into a little more detail on what each app is specifically used for.

Redfin

For someone who is not a Real Estate agent with direct access to the MLS, Redfin is probably the next best thing. From my experience I've found Redfin to be the most up-to-date and accurate from all the other places MLS listings are posted. I've tried other's including Zillow, but I've consistently ran into old and outdated posts as well as some that appeared to be scams. The app itself is also extremely user friendly when you're adjusting your filters and makes saving your searches and favorite listings super easy to do. So if you're looking for a potential property on the MLS, please utilize Redfin over everything else. Also, if you don't have an agent you're already working with, Redfin offers great flexibility with agents available directly through them. So if you see a listing on the app and would like to check it out that same day, chances are Redfin will have an available agent for you.

Zillow

Zillow is a great platform – Redfin definitely beats them out when it comes to homes for sale, but they have many other great features that work incredibly well for someone who is trying to self-manage rental properties!

I'll start with just the regular Zillow application. I pull rent comparisons all the time for the markets and area's I'm interested in even if I don't currently have any open rentals on the market. This is extremely important because it allows you to keep pace with what's going on in the marketplace. It also prepares you to make the right moves when it comes to your rent renewals for the tenants you currently do have in place. For example, let's say I just signed a new tenant to a 1-year lease for $2,000 a month for a 3-bedroom single family home. 10-12 months later when it's time to renew their lease, do you think I would raise the rent if the rent comparison for 3-bedroom single family homes in the area were ranging between $1800-1900? What if the cheapest 3-bedroom single family home was now renting for $2,300? Knowing this information in the areas you're investing in are critical and leveraging all the free information Zillow offers is a great option.

Zillow – Rental Manager

Another great app from the Zillow tree is their Rental Manager offerings. This allows you the ability to post a listing, send out tenant applications along with background/credit checks, sign new state specific leases, and collect monthly rent. I use all of these except the collect rent option which is a personal choice which I will get into later for another app on the list. Not only is listing your rental free, but it also gets posted to their affiliate pages which includes Trulia and Hot Pads. You can literally reach thousands of people within a few clicks. Secondly, the application process is painless for your future tenant. They see the listing on Zillow, and they directly apply on Zillow. There is no paperwork you have to worry about printing or documents you have to request. And last but not least, the part that I feel sets Zillow apart from the rest is the state specific lease signings they offer directly from your listing. These are not generic, and they take into account any and all state specific laws that might apply where you are located. If you print a random generic lease off the internet and you're not familiar with all of your states law's, you could be in for a ton of trouble down the line. That is why I love using Zillow for this because I know they have everything covered. You're also able to get everything electronically signed within a couple minutes which also speeds up the entire process.

Zillow – 3D Home

The third and final Zillow influenced application I use is one of their newer ones called 3D Home. This feature became a big deal during the COVID lockdown period throughout 2020 because people did not feel comfortable walking into another person's house. This 3D Home feature allows you to take full 360 angle videos with your phone so any potential tenant viewing your listing can get a real feel for what the property looks like. Another great advantage to using this feature is it spotlights your listing when you're looking at the Zillow map. Most listings don't currently take advantage of this feature so when you're viewing the listings on the map and you see one that stands out with the highlight "3D Home" it leads to more clicks!

Hot Pads and Facebook Marketplace

Combining these 2 together because I use them for the exact same thing. You can never have too many platforms for researching comparable rents. I routinely will log in once a week or so and see if there are any new listings in the area's I'm looking to buy. Please keep in mind you have to be very specific with what you're looking for down to the square footage, bedroom count, etc. Otherwise you're just going to be wasting your time. For example, currently I'm specifically looking for 2-bedroom 1 bath around 800 square foot units to see how much the rents are going for. I have it this narrowed down because I plan on my next purchase to be a duplex with each unit being similar to those numbers. Because I know exactly what I'm looking for, pulling up this app and looking for comparable rentals takes me no longer than 2 minutes to do and I'm not wasting my time.

QuickBooks

From all 12 apps I listed above, QuickBooks is the only one that I pay for but in my opinion it is worth the $20 monthly subscription. When it comes to accounting and keeping all the numbers for your rental properties in order, I don't see a better option out there. If you're just getting started or just have 1-2 rentals it might seem like you can manage everything from a notepad on your desk, or a little excel file you keep everything on and that might be okay for now. As you grow and add more units to your portfolio, you're going to need a more streamlined way to see how your properties are performing and QuickBooks offers that in a very user-friendly way. In a matter of a few clicks I can pull up what my Balance Sheet and my Profit/Loss statement and highlight how much each property is producing or not producing. Also, most accountants are very well versed at using QuickBooks, and the webpage actually has a feature where you can give your accountant access to pull whatever documents are needed. Aside from all the money reports available, you're also able to send your tenants easy electronic invoicing every month that makes it easy for them to pay their rent.

Thumbtack

One of the biggest concerns most people have when deciding to buy a rental property is how they're going to get repairs and maintenance issues resolved when they arise without it being a headache. If you have a property manager they would obviously be handling this, but most people starting out don't want to pay 10% for a property manager and decide to self-manage. I've used many different apps, I've used Yelp, and good old google searches when looking for general maintenance help or even a specific skilled technician but most have sucked. Thumbtack is the only one that has consistently come through for me when I needed help. I've found electricians, plumbers, handyman, landscapers, and many others. I've hired in all these different areas for work on rental property that I own, and I haven't been disappointed. SO if you're worried about not knowing who you'd call in case something needed to be repaired, don't worry because chances are they're on Thumbtack ready to be hired.

Tiny Scanner

This is a simple one. Chances are at some point you're going to need to send someone a piece of document you have laying around at the house with no electronic copy saved on your computer. Taking a picture of the document will not be sufficient for banks. In comes Tiny Scanner. The app allows you to take a picture of whatever document you need to send, and it converts it to look like you put it through the office scanner. This puts a professional touch on the document and saves a trip to some scanning store you'd otherwise have to go to. If you have an iPhone, the recent iOS updates might have made it possible to do something similar with the notes app so you may not even need something like this.

Credit Karma

This is the best app I've used to track my credit. Nowadays the market is saturated with the amount of ways you can track your credit. From your online banking to your credit card providers, everyone has some form of way for you to check your credit score. In my experience Credit Karma has provided the most useful information and its free. You're able to see all your open accounts very easily, how you stack up against all the different metrics that weigh your overall score, and it updates on a weekly basis. If you're someone who cares about their credit, and this should be everyone, Credit Karma is a great way to keep track to make sure you're ready to make that rental purchase!

Home Depot

This one is by no means necessary but I've found it very helpful, especially when I purchased a place that needed some work. Having the Home Depot app handy to see how much things cost as you're walking a property is a really great practice. Additionally, even though this isn't something I've taken advantage of just yet, Home Depot has a better partnership with contractors. Mostly whatever you want to buy and install, Home Depot has the option to hire a "professional" to do the work as well which I think is what separates them from Lowe's.

Chase

Finally, Chase is what I use for my mobile banking for my rental properties. Now I don't care if you use Chase specifically, but the main takeaway I want you to have is to separate your rental property income/expense from your personal with a bank that has all the electronic features. For many years I kept my rental property and personal income combined in one account and it was extremely unorganized. My only gauge on whether or not I was making more money was if the account had more money in it than it did the previous month. That my friends is not someone who is on top of their financials so don't be that person. Have a separate account for your business to help keep you organized and help keep better track of your finances. Also, as I mentioned before make sure the bank you choose is in the 21st century with their electronic options. There are going to be times where you need to deposit a check, transfer money, etc. and nowadays that should not require you to take time out of your day to go to the bank. You should be able to do everything with your cell phone so make sure the bank gives you that flexibility.

Chapter Summary:
- Yes, you can utilize your mobile device and the internet for more than just social media. Use it as a tool to learn.
- With everything you need at your fingertips, there is absolutely no reason to make excuses on why you can't jump into real estate investing.

Chapter 7

Flipping vs. Buy and Hold

"Don't buy things you can't afford with money you don't have to impress people you don't like."

Dave Ramsey

I love In-n-Out burgers. If you don't know what that is look it up because you're missing out on life, and not to mention the animal style fries! Right about now you might be asking yourself why the heck I'm here talking about a burger when you want to read about flipping vs. holding property. Well let me tell you... I want you to picture having a brand new built In-n-Out right across the street from your house, and if you don't know what In-n-Out is picture the best burger place you've ever had. If you don't eat meat picture the best impossible burger you've ever had. Yeah that's right, we're here to please everyone (not really).

Now with the most amazing burger place right across from you, I want you to picture the CEO walking across the street and knocking on your door. You open your front door looking pleasantly surprised to see the CEO of your favorite burger place standing right there. He looks you dead in the eyes and says, "listen... We've decided to give you everything we have on our menu for free today." You jump for joy, maybe even shed a few tears, and accept his gracious offer. You call over all your friends and enjoy an amazing meal, maybe even save some leftovers in the fridge for the next day. Morning comes and you wake up with a smile on your face still shocked at this incredible gesture by the CEO of your favorite burger restaurant. You walk outside your door to check your mail, and the burger restaurant is gone! Its vanished. You have no idea what happened, but it seems the whole restaurant just disappeared over night. You feel distraught, anxious, and just down-right sad. You go out driving around looking for another restaurant of your favorite burger place because now you're just hooked and you need more just to survive another day! This my friends is what you get when you're flipping houses. You get that instant big win, but then it's all gone, and you must go after another one. It's a job. The whole reason why we preach investing in Real Estate is so you don't have to worry about having a job. In our little dramatic story above, if we were talking about buy and hold real estate for the long-term, that burger spot would maybe not offer us the whole menu on day 1, but it would stay there giving us a free meal every single day till WE decided we wanted to stop having some. That right there is the difference.

You see flipping vs. buy and hold Real Estate might both be in the real estate world, so people assume they are similar but in reality they are totally different things. Let's take some time to go over each one.

Buy and Hold

When you're investing in buy and hold real estate you're doing so for the long-term. Your time horizon should be 5+ years at the bare minimum. There are obviously exit strategies you can take if certain circumstances change, but when you're going into a deal you need to be thinking for the future. The two catalyst's that should be driving your decision making is the monthly cash flow you're going to be creating, and the probabilities of appreciation over your long-term holding period. In addition to these two driving forces, with buy and hold properties you also get the tax benefits every year and the ability to have someone else (your tenant) pay down your loan which ultimately increases your net worth every single month.

Buy and hold is also extremely more passive than flipping is. Don't get me wrong, it's not going to be completely passive like some would make you believe. There is still work that you need to do whether its dealing with the tenants directly or managing your property manager to make sure they are doing everything correctly. Either way, if you are doing everything by the book, buy and hold will allow you the level of passivity to live your life the way you choose to live it.

One thing that's extremely similar between the two is making sure you get your math right. For buy and hold the math going into the deal is everything. You need to remember this is something you're locking yourself into for the long-term, so if you get the math wrong and jump into a bad deal it's going to impact you for years. Getting the math right at the beginning is also where you're going to make most of your money. By getting yourself into a good deal from the beginning, you're ensuring you have great monthly cash flow from the start, and if you did your homework and picked a good location, you have set yourself up for long-term wealth over time through appreciation.

Flipping

Conversely, when you're flipping home's you're doing so for the short-term with a time horizon between 3-6 months. Flipping is not investing. It's similar to having a 9-5 job. I mentioned the numbers being important for both, but it's even more critical when you're planning on flipping a home. If you get the numbers wrong, you do not have the luxury of holding the property for the long-term and allowing it time to appreciate. You're going to end up selling for a loss and taking a big hit if you did not forecast properly so you absolutely need to be careful here and do the math. Additionally, many people flipping homes use hard money lenders because they're easier and quicker to work with and most conventional banks aren't going to finance your short-term flip. When you're flipping home's you also don't get to take advantage of the yearly tax benefits like deprecation, and you don't get to build long-term wealth through appreciation and loan pay down.

With all that being said, flipping home's is a great way to generate a good amount of cash in a short amount of time. If you find a good deal and run your numbers properly, you can make a lot of money flipping homes all year round. But one thing will never change... Once you're done with a flip the money coming is dried up. You now need to do it again, and again, and again. This is why the analogy between flipping and a 9-5 comes up because you need to keep doing it in order to keep making money from it.

In my opinion, the question isn't which one is better than the other. It really depends on what your goals are... For the purpose of this book, we're talking about financial freedom and you get financial freedom by creating enough passive income so you don't have to work anymore. So if my personal goal is to reach financial freedom, flipping homes doesn't necessarily help me. I need to add more buy and hold properties to my portfolio which will result in more monthly passive cash flow and long- term wealth building through appreciation and loan pay down.

If your goal is to find a way to make a living by generating cash in a shorter time horizon then maybe flipping is for you.

But again, flipping is not investing. It's a source of income similar to a 9-5 job.

In a perfect world the two would be fueling each other. You can make a lot of money flipping homes and the profits generated by your flips will then in turn fund your long-term buy and hold real estate. By the two working together, you're able to generate cash with your flips to help feed your family and also put some to the side. Then when you have enough put aside you can go out and purchase a rental property that will start generating monthly passive income for you. You see the goal at the end of the day is still to create enough monthly cash flow so you don't have to work anymore. I am essentially doing the same thing in my life right now as I write this book, but instead of using flipping homes as a way to feed myself and put some money aside, I'm using a 9-5 job. This is again how flipping and a 9-5 are similar.

As we wrap up this chapter, I will hit you with one more analogy between the two and it's in regard to the stock market. I feel like this is relevant in today's world because we have so many more people investing their money now, albeit not all with the right mindset. Warren buffet is a long-term investor. He made his billions by purchasing companies at low depressed levels, and over-time made a shit load of money because he just allowed time to do what it does. Through the economy growing and inflation playing its role, his money grew exponentially. This is similar to buy and hold real estate. If you buy right and give it time, you are essentially guaranteeing yourself a wealthy future. Flipping homes is more like day trading. You need to be in front of your screen staring at the price every single day. Once you get a good trade in and make some money, you have to be on the hunt for the next stock. It never ends, and again, it's like having another job.

Don't get infatuated with flipping homes because you see a big pay day at the end. Instead, if you want to flip homes try and see how the cash from flipping a home can fuel your long-term investing strategy so that you don't have to work anymore.

Chapter Summary:
- Flipping homes and buying a rental property are two completely different things.
- Flipping is like having a 9-5 job that earns you money.
- Rental property is passive income that allows you to take advantage of appreciation, tax advantageous, and loan pay down.
- If you want them to work together, you need to utilize the cash earned from flipping homes to fund your rental property purchases just like you would if you had an actual 9-5 w2 job.

Chapter 8

Math > Love

"Every decision you make takes you one step closer to being wealthy… or one step further away.

Shay Olivarria

Maybe if there was a mathematical way to find a life partner we'd have less divorces in today's world. To be honest, I'm surprised this doesn't exist yet. Take a test, donate your blood, have some scientists run some more tests, and BOOM you have your perfect match. I'd support this personally because frankly how many times can you tell someone what your favorite color is? Send help. Anyways I digress…

This is exactly why my first love is and always will be Real Estate because you can take all emotions out of it, do the math, and ensure it's the perfect match for you before you move forward. Doing the math is what takes the fear out of investing. Most people don't invest because of the fear they have deep inside about losing their hard-earned money. What if the market crashes? What if I lose my job? Isn't a 401k safer? These are the questions people ask themselves and the answers in their head terrifies them to the point where they don't even give it a second thought. I can tell you right now with all the confidence in the world, investing in Real Estate is probably one of the safest investments you can make as long as you do the math.

In this chapter I want to talk about cash-on-cash return. There are many ways to calculate whether an investment is a good or bad deal, and anyone looking to purchase a property should do their research. The scope of this book is to highlight how simple Real Estate investing can be, and therefore we will only cover cash-on-cash return because if you nail down just this one math problem, you will already be miles ahead of everyone else looking to get started with their first investment.

In order to calculate cash on cash return properly we need to understand a couple terms and their definitions.

Cash flow – The monthly profit left over after you take out all the expenses and debt. So if you own a single-family house and you collect $3,200 in rent, then you subtract the mortgage you owe to the bank, property taxes, interest, insurance, and any other misc. expense you might have. Let's say after all these expenses are paid, you're left with $778. This is what your monthly cash flow is. See the diagram on the next page to get a visual of what this looks like.

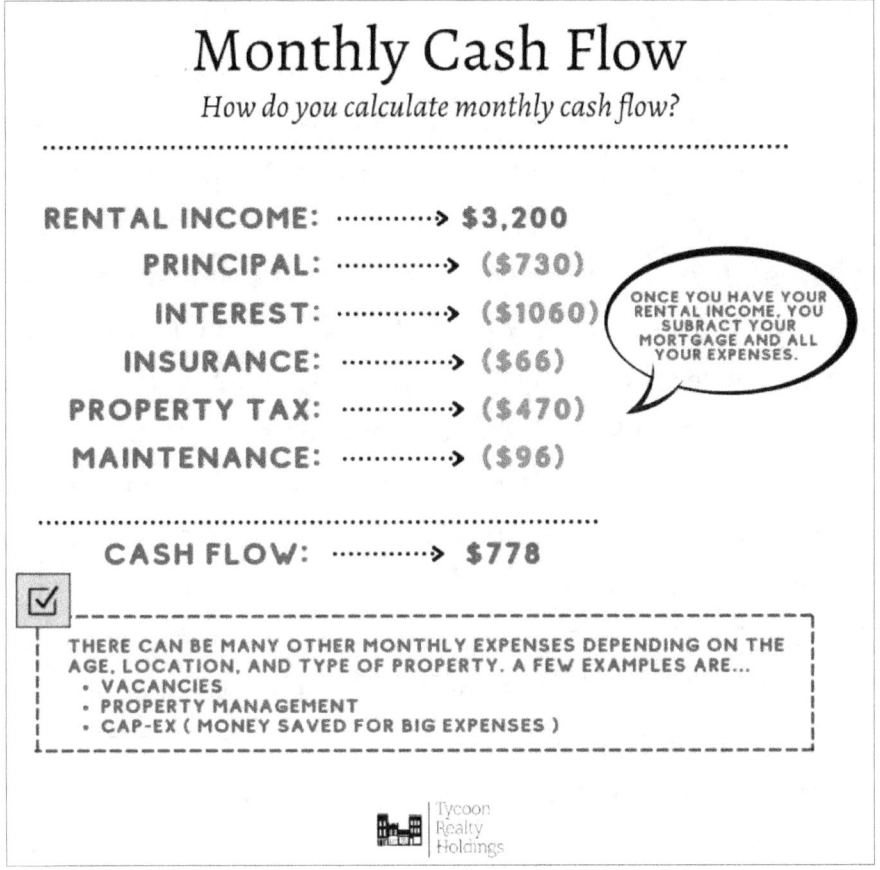

Cash-on-Cash Return – Now that we know what our cash flow is, we can calculate our cash-on-cash return. By definition your cash-on-cash return is your total annual cash flow divided by the total amount of cash you need to spend to purchase the property. Let's say you purchased a property for $400,000 and put 20% as a down payment which is $80,000. You typically will have closing costs and as the buyer lets estimate this to be an additional $5,000. So total into this deal you would have to put in $85,000 cash out of your pocket. Using the example from our cash flow definition let's say you estimate your monthly profit to be $778 which over a course of 12 months would be $9,336. All you have to do now is take that $9,336 and divide it by $85,000 which will give us 10.9%. Your cash-on-cash return annually for this investment would be 10.9%. That is how simple it is, and you can easily do this for any listing you see on the MLS.

Before jumping on Redfin and busting out your calculator you need to ask yourself what type of return do I want to see on my investment? This is where your financial knowledge needs to come into play and if you don't know the answer it's OKAY – Truth is there is no right answer, and everyone has to figure out what works for them. What you should do is take all the information that's public knowledge and ask yourself what you feel most comfortable with. Let's look at what we all know when it comes to the rate of return on other investments.

Savings Account – Less than 1%

CD Accounts – 1-2%

401K Account – 5-8%

Under your Mattress – 0% - Technically its less than 0% when you factor inflation. Get out the drug game kids.

These are the most common places people stash their money and the averages are typical of what you would see annually for each. Knowing this information you can now easily ask yourself, what amount of return would I be satisfied with if I purchased a rental property? Once you answer that question, you can hop on the MLS, find multiple listings that catch your eye and do the math!

Aside from the cash-on-cash return, you have to understand with Real Estate the money you're making doesn't stop there. Your property is more than likely going to appreciate around 3-5% a year. That's money YOU'RE making. The tenant is going to pay down the loan for you. Again, that is YOUR net worth that's increasing every single month your loan gets paid. All the other investments you're putting your money into do not give you the same amount of wealth building opportunities. If you buy a rental property and in 5 years' time the property is worth $100,000 more than what you paid for it, the loan has been paid down by $25k, and you raised your rent by $200 a month, is your cash-on-cash return still the same as when you purchased the property? The answer is absolutely not. At some point your annual returns become LIMITLESS! Everything you make is pure profit because you've already made your initial investment back. You're playing with the house's money but in this game the house does not win. YOU win.

Chapter Summary:
- Real estate does not care about your emotions. It is important to take an analytical approach. Run your numbers and decide whether it has the potential to be a great deal or not.
- Correctly estimate your cash flow using realistic numbers. Many people will fudge the numbers to make it work just because they like a property. Be realistic.
- Decide what type of cash on cash return you are comfortable with and willing to accept. What is your money making right now wherever you have it stored?

Chapter 9

Out of State vs. Local Investing

> *"Be thankful for what you have; you'll end up having more. If you concentrate on what you don't have, you will never... have enough."*
>
> Oprah Winfrey

Over the course of the last couple years the Real Estate market has been on fire! If I could insert emoji's here it would call for at least 10 fire emoji's because that's how hot the market has been. There are multiple markets across the country that are seeing double digit year over year appreciation, which is amazing for anyone who owns property, but it could be extremely devasting for someone living in a super expensive market and trying to purchase a property, especially if they are just starting out. Full transparency here I have never purchased an out of state property – I own properties in multiple state's but I've only purchased in the state that I've been living in at the time. I warn you of this because everything I have to say on this topic is strictly my opinion from my personal experience. Also, there is no right answer when it comes to out of state vs. local investing. Everyone's situation is different and you can be successful no matter which route you decide to go. I'm here to try and explain what I see as the pros and cons to each one with a bias to local investing.

For starters, the number 1 reason why I see people trying to invest out of state in a completely different market is because of the cheaper home values. I absolutely hate this reason and I think it's the worst possible reason to purchase a rental property. I wonder if those same people thinking about purchasing in a completely different state just because of home prices ever stop and ask themselves, "hey, maybe it's cheaper there for a reason???"

I have a cousin named Sarkis who lives in Philadelphia, and he has been trying to convince me to purchase property with him in the Philadelphia area for some time now. According to him there has been increased property development with new construction everywhere and property values have been steadily increasing. You can probably purchase a property in his neighborhood for under 200k easy. This price range is pretty close to what you can expect to find in most of the Midwest of the country as well as the Sun Belt outside of California. Now I love my cousin but he's probably not going to like what I have to say next. Who the hell wants to live in Philadelphia? Freezing cold winters and broken-down buildings everywhere. If anything, people are moving out of Philadelphia.

Now let's try and breakdown some of the pros and cons here so you can understand why I feel the way I feel about this. Pros - Can you buy a property for less than 200k? Yes, sure you can. Can you rent that property and make a good profit every month with solid cash flow? Maybe. As great as those two sound, in my opinion the cons outweigh the pros. Cons – good luck finding a good tenant. It's possible, but your chances of running into a bad tenant that will ruin your investment is extremely higher in cities that don't have great employment numbers. This is because businesses aren't moving to these states. You might have good colleges with a solid student base but guess what? Those college kids are leaving the second they graduate to a warmer nicer place in the country. Additionally, you will not see anywhere close to the same amount of appreciation in these markets. Real wealth is not made by collecting monthly rent. Real wealth is made in Appreciation of your property. The properties in Philadelphia might increase in value from 150k to 200k – Congrats you made 50k over a 5-year period. But that home in California, as expensive as it is, is going to go from 500k to 750k during the same time period. This doesn't mean you have to buy an expensive property in California, but you need to be in a market that is going to see strong appreciation and the truth is most of these states that have extremely cheap home prices do not see the same amount of appreciation. What if you're someone who lives in these states? Does that mean you shouldn't invest where you are? Not exactly – because there is one factor that outweighs everything mentioned above.

Aside from the smaller good tenant pool in these states which will lead to high turnover rates and the less chances of appreciation, there are two other big factors that make out of state investing the most challenging which conversely makes it okay if you're someone who is local to the area. You must pay someone to watch over your property. You must have some sort of boots on the ground since you're not going to be able to do it from thousands of miles away. And this is the reason why it might be okay for someone living in those smaller states to still find a good deal and make a purchase. In today's world, you would have to pay a property manager around 10% of the rental income you're collecting. So, if you rent a home for $2,000, two hundred of that is going to the property manager. This will destroy your monthly cash flow and can turn a good investment into a bad one. This is the biggest advantage a person has when they self-manage. Unless you're buying a property that is 20+ units, the cash flow coming in is not going to be high enough to afford a property manager in most cases.

The second reason is financing. Investing locally allows you to purchase a property as a primary residence with great financing terms and turn it into a rental. This is often referred to "house hacking." You can house hack in a couple different ways. One way is living in the property for a year, and then deciding to move on to another property while turning the original one into a rental. Another way is deciding to rent the additional rooms you have in the house while you live there as well. You can also do this if the home has an ADU (Accessory Dwelling Units). Many dense metro cities have ADU additions to the home which can create a great opportunity to house hack, and the potential for additional rental income down the line. The interest rate difference between primary and investment properties can be huge. Right now, you can get a primary residence loan for about 3% where an investment property will run you around 4%. That is a big gap. You also have the flexibility to put anywhere between 5-20% as a down payment for a primary residence on a conventional loan, when an investment loan will require at least 20-25%. This again is a big gap.

House hacking is a great strategy to slowly grow a rental portfolio without needing to save 20% for a down payment every time you want to buy a property. In fact, there is data that shows the average down payment is only 12% so don't believe the false misconception that you need to save 20%. Obviously, the less of a down payment you put, the higher your payment will be, so you still need to be able to qualify for the mortgage. Additionally, if you put anything less than 20% as a down payment you will have to pay extra insurance every single month. This is called PMI (Private Mortgage

Insurance). This is an additional layer of insurance you must pay because you are seen as someone who has a higher risk of defaulting on their loan since you were not able to put at least 20% down. The monthly PMI payment is usually not much but it's something you still need to consider. The PMI payment will automatically falloff once you've hit 20% of equity in the home. Depending on the lender, you can also pay for an appraisal and if the new appraised value of the home is way higher than what you purchased it for making it so you have at least 20% equity in the property, they will remove the PMI payment.

In summary, most people who are looking to invest out of state are people who live in expensive cities and are looking for a more affordable price point. They have this false sense of attraction when they see a property in the middle of nowhere that's pennies on the dollar compared to where they live. You'll rarely see the opposite where someone who lives in an already cheap real estate market and is looking to invest somewhere where prices are expensive. I'm here to tell you to not get suckered into this. Those homes are cheap for a reason. You need to do your homework and not just invest because a market looks cheap. There are going to be markets that catch fire at times and have great population growth which will as a result drive strong appreciation as well. At this current time in 2021 Texas and Florida are great examples of this. You have to take that research and see if paying someone 10% off the top plus dishing out at least a 20% down payment still makes a property a good deal. I personally rather pay more for a property that is in a city that I'm currently living in and not worry about paying someone 10% to care for it for me, plus get better financing terms because guess what? That person doesn't care about your property. It is not theirs and it's not their equity. They're just there to collect their paycheck every month and go about the rest of their day. So, if you're looking to purchase a small 1-4-unit property, I do not recommend buying out of state unless its driving distance. You're the only person who is going to care enough to grow this business you're creating and the last thing you want is to put it in the hands of some stranger. One day when you are a Real Estate tycoon and have hundreds of units and are taking home great monthly income, you can discuss the potential for hiring out some of the property management work. If you're just getting started or even have a handful of units, I do not recommend it!

Okay so what if you live in an expensive market and you also don't want to pay 10% for a property manager to invest somewhere far away or put down a hefty down payment, does that mean you just shouldn't be buying anything? Absolutely NOT! We will go further into this topic in the next chapter, Opportunities in any market.

Chapter Summary:
- When you're first starting out, it's important to learn the entire process of a rental from buying the property to managing it.
- I do not suggest paying 10% of your rent collected to someone to manage for you because it's going to take too big of a chunk out of your profits and some stranger is not going to care about your 1-unit property as much as you are.
- Local investing allows you to house hack and purchase properties with great financing terms which make barrier to entry much easier.
- Once you become a more sophisticated investor and have more units, a property manager is something you can slowly transition into.

Chapter 10

Opportunities in Any Market

"There are some people who live in a dream world, and there are some who face reality; and then there are those who turn one into the other."

Douglas H. Everett

Why are people so afraid of sub-markets? It's almost like they rather invest in something blindly that's across the country, than invest in something that's within a few hours' drive of them. I have regular conversations about real estate with my friends and I've noticed so often we end up talking about markets in completely different states than the ones we live in. It seems like there is this weird and unique attraction to want to invest in a different state far away because the prices seem to look attractive or because we heard of someone else who bought somewhere else and had good things to say about it. The truth is you don't need to invest thousands of miles away even if the market you're in is too expensive. After sitting down and really thinking about why myself and others feel this way, I feel as though I figured out the answer and I'm going to share it with you here.

I grew up around Southern California mostly in the Los Angeles County area. We lived in the "valley" which is pretty much some of the suburbs of LA County. You have pockets in the valley that might be considered crappy areas, but for the most part relatively speaking the valley offers good safe neighborhoods. The valley is also not cheap – Recently looking at the MLS, it's hard to find any single-family home that's under $650,000. So naturally, whoever is living in this type of expensive market might look elsewhere if they were looking to buy a rental property investment. So as a result, they start to think about investing in Texas, Arizona, maybe even as far away as Florida because those places sound exotic and sexy and they've also heard how great these places are for investing from people on social media, podcasts, and other social avenues. Don't get me wrong, there is valid truth to investing in an up-and-coming city and place – But if you're just starting out this should not be your first step. Hell, it shouldn't even be your 5th step. If you are in the valley, you can drive 1-3 hours out and find cheap ass real estate in places like Bakersfield or somewhere like Victorville. Why don't people think about these places? Because they are not nice. They are not sexy. They know this because they've driven by these cities and places and have seen what they look like with their own two eyes, so they are automatically dismissive of them. If you're someone who is reading this book let me ask you a question. Who cares? Are you going to be living there your whole life? No. So again, who cares? Do you think the homes in those other states are going to appreciate faster than the sub-markets in California? Nope, I doubt it.

My point here being is there are opportunities in any market that you're living in, even if that means you maybe have to drive a little to get there.

Chapter Summary:
- Do not get infatuated with investing thousands of miles away just because of something you saw or heard.
- No matter how expensive your market is, chances are there are sub-markets within driving distance that will make investing easier
- Sub-markets near expensive cities will do just as good if not better than a cheap city in the middle of nowhere.
- When people get priced out of expensive cities that they have lived in for years, most do not relocate to another state. They drive down to the closest city they can afford. This is one of the selling points to investing in sub-markets near expensive cities.

Chapter 11

Passive Income > Earned Income

"In investing, what is comfortable is rarely profitable."

Robert Arnott

What would happen if you lost your job today? How long would you be able to support yourself or your family if you lost your paycheck? The number one issue I see with everyone around me is they're chasing the wrong dream because of what they've been taught growing up their whole lives. They have the completely wrong idea about what financial independence really means. Ask 100 people what their financial goals currently are, and I bet you 99 of them would talk about getting their salary increased to "x" amount at their current place of employment. Or maybe tell you about how they would want to work for so and so employer making "x" amount per year.

Who cares how much you're making a year if you're working for someone else? I'm not necessarily saying this is always a bad thing, but the truth is you could be let go at any time. The company could go under at any time. Your profession could become obsolete because of future innovations. No one plans for stuff like this – they just assume that paycheck is always going to be there. And even if it is, why are you okay working 40-50 hours a week till your 65 years old just to retire? When most people think of retiring, they automatically associate it with old age. Why do you have to be old to retire? Maybe because that's what your 9th grade teacher taught you in high school. Having a job that pays you a decent salary is not a bad thing, but you must have an exit strategy in place. Over the last 8 years my 9-5 job has helped fuel my Real Estate portfolio because I've had a strategy in place. My strategy wasn't to sit back and live paycheck to paycheck till I was old and wrinkled. I put a plan in place that would allow me to save enough money to fund my next property and I repeated this step over and over again and I am still doing it today as I write this book. Purchasing that first property is the hardest step. I guarantee you 99.9% of people out there who have purchased at least 1 property as a buy and hold rental have not stopped at just one. They've continued to build and add more properties because of all the benefits that came along with that first purchase. In this chapter I want to break down the difference between passive income vs. earned income to show everyone why passive income is so important.

First lets breakdown what passive income and earned income really mean for you.

Earned Income
- You trade your time for money. Like working an hourly/salary job.
  - This could also be true if you own a business. If you own a business but are working 10 hours a day, you're trading your time for money.
- High Taxes
  - Working in an hourly/salaried job includes paying your state and federal taxes straight from your paycheck. In some state this could be 30% of your earned income. Government gets paid first and you have very little control.

Passive Income
- You are not actively trading your time for money.
  - When you own a rental property, the tenant will be paying you rent every month and you don't have to leave your couch. How active you want to be is up to you. You can hire a property manager to take any phone calls if things arise, or you can handle them yourself. Nevertheless, this is not a daily time-consuming activity and you're not trading your time for money.
- Low Taxes
  - Passive income streams like real estate allow you to write off all your expenses before you pay your taxes. By the time all the expenses are written off, there is very little remaining to be taxed on. Government gets paid last and you have control.

Now that you have a clear understanding of what each one means wouldn't you rather have your main income source be passive income? Of-course the answer should be yes. The question is how you get there. If a young 22-year-old kid making $15 an hour can get there, so can you. Fear is the number one reason why people in this game don't get started. Fear of losing their money. I'm about to fill everyone in on a little secret. When you put your money into a purchase of a home, your money is not lost. Its sitting there in the equity of your property. But unlike a savings account making you less than pennies on the dollar, the money in this property is going to be making you monthly cash flow, give you tax benefits, chances of appreciation, and someone else is going to be paying your monthly mortgage. Your money is not lost. It's just sitting in there making you filthy rich.

Everyone's financial goal in life should include being able to support themselves and their family strictly through passive income. This is how you retire early, and you don't need to create the next best technology application out there to do it. That's why I love Real Estate. It doesn't matter who you are, how smart or dumb you are, anyone can make the life decision to buy a rental property.

Chapter Summary:
- Earned income gets taxed at the highest rate.
- Passive income allows you to write off all your expenses first, and tax only what is left over.
- Don't be okay with working 4 months out of the year for the government with none of that hard earned income ever making it into your bank account.
- Everyone's goal should be working towards getting your passive income to surpass what your earned income currently is and the best way to do that is through real estate.

Chapter 12

Uncle Sam

"How many millionaires do you know who have become wealthy by investing in savings accounts? I rest my case."

Robert G. Allen

There are so many people out there with 9-5 w2 jobs who absolutely don't care how much taxes they are paying with every single paycheck. They've somehow convinced themselves that they are paying their fair share and doing their part to help others or some bull shit like this – I'm not exactly sure so you might need to go out there and find someone who thinks this way to get all the facts right. They won't be too hard to find I promise.

Listen, I'm all for chipping in and doing my part, but the truth is many people in our society simply just don't have the education when it comes to taxes to understand what is right vs. wrong and what they can actually do about it. Hell, I bet you your own tax accountant doesn't know all the ins and outs neither! I myself am by no means a tax expert so I'm not going to pretend to be, but I have learned all the amazing tax advantageous that real estate investments will offer you and that is what I will focus on here.

For starters there is a huge difference between how you are taxed at your 9-5 job vs. how you are taxed on your real estate investments. I experience this first-hand as I've worked and continue to work in 2 of the highest income tax states being California and Oregon. I gross around 40K more annually at my 9-5 job right now vs. what I make in rental income with my real estate portfolio, but at the end of the day after you take all the taxes out, I net more from my real estate investments than I do from my 9-5 job. Isn't that mind blowing crazy?!? I couldn't believe it when I did the math. I really considered walking in and quitting my job after realizing this because all I could think about every single day was how many days and hours I was spending busting my ass at work to give my money to the government. I was literally working 4-5 months out of the year and not seeing a penny of it touch my bank account. How do people just blindly accept this? Well, it's probably mainly because they feel they don't have another choice. Let me tell you right now, outside of moving to a state with no income tax, which still only covers a quarter of what's taken out of your check, this book is your choice. This book is how you achieve your financial independence and stop forking over 4 months of your hard work to the government every single year.

I'll stop my ranting now and get back to the point. When you're working your w2 job, the government gets paid first, and you get paid last. When its tax season everyone sits around and can't wait to get their refund in the mail – Do you know WHY you get a refund every year? Because the government took too much money from you. They took more than they should have, and they are giving you YOUR money back to you and we get all happy about it. That money should have never even been taken out of your check in the first place, so I don't think it's a cause for celebration when you get your refund. It should be a red flag and get you to start thinking differently about your finances.

Our government and tax code really support real estate and all the tax breaks they give us is not an accident. There is a reason why real estate investors are given all these great advantageous – two reasons to be exact. Reason 1: Have you ever seen government housing? They're nasty. Go to any communist country where the government oversees all the housing projects, and you'll see exactly what I mean. They're trash because the government doesn't do a great job in upkeeping the properties. Therefore, they love real estate investors because investors update properties and provide proper housing to people looking to rent, and they don't have to worry about it. Reason 2: Investors take out massive mortgage loans. When an investor takes out hundreds of thousands on a loan, that money/debt is created and gives a boost to the overall economy. These 2 reasons are why real estate investors get these tax breaks from the government.

There are no shady or illegal things you need to do to take advantage of the tax code – I only say this because when uneducated people hear of wealthy millionaires who own businesses and real estate not paying much in taxes, they get all upset and think the system is rigged. The only reason they believe the system is rigged is because they don't know any better. If they just took the time to learn a little more about how money works, they would not only make better financial decisions, but they will also not look at the successful business owners with such hate just because of how much money the person makes. There is a laundry list of real line items you can write off when you own a rental property, but for the sake of time I'm only going to spend some time going over the main one's. Again, I am not an accountant or a tax professional so please seek the advice of a professional before taking any action yourself.

- Property taxes
- Mortgage interest
- Mortgage insurance
- Repairs and maintenance
- Depreciation of the property
- Deprecation of appliances
- Mileage
- Property management

- Utilities
- HOA fee's

This list will be the most common write off items for the majority of people out there. Most people are aware about being able to write off their property taxes and their interest, but the biggest one that everyone needs to know about is deprecation. The tax code allows you to take your rental property, split the value between the land and the building, then depreciate whatever the value of the building is for 27.5 years. Also, this is something that you have to do according to the tax code. It's not like you have the option not to depreciate your property if you don't want to. Let's walk through an easy example… Let's say you purchased a home for $500,000 and after discussing it with your accountant you've determined from the $500,000 you paid for the property, 100k is the value of the land and $400,000k is the value of the building. Your accountant would then take $400,000 and divide that by 27.5 which would equal $14,545. So for the next twenty-seven and a half years you will automatically write off $14,545 from your one rental property every single year. That is a shit ton of money to write off for just deprecation. When you consider your property taxes, interest, insurance, and everything else listed above, you're going to have thousands and thousands worth in legal write offs for every property that you have.

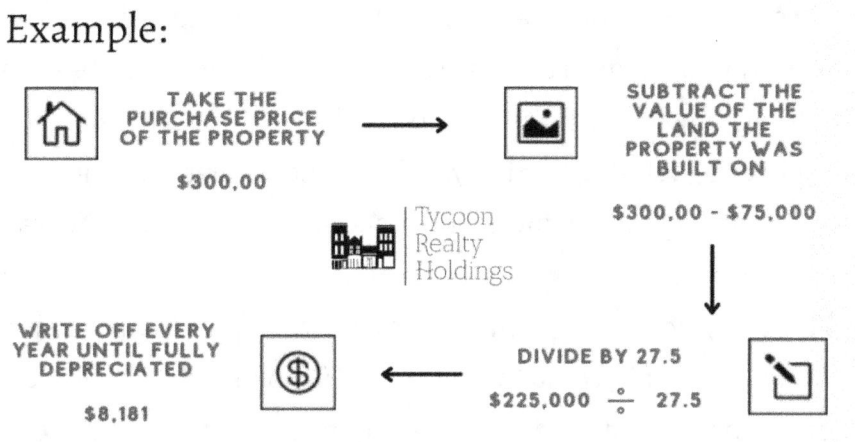

- Depreciation is one of the biggest tax write offs for rental property owners
- Depreciation of a rental property is not optional
- Deprecation alone will offset your rental income, resulting in little to no taxes owed

This is why investors who own many properties don't have to pay much in taxes. It's not like they're getting away with something sneaky. It's just a matter of being smart with your money. I encourage everyone who owns real estate or is thinking about getting into real estate to buy "The Book on Tax Strategies" by Amanda Han and Matthew MacFarland. They do an amazing job going through all the tax write offs you can claim and give real life examples of their clients who have already gone through all the hurdles so you don't have to. I also recommend you pay for an actual accountant and not attempt to do this on your own in TurboTax. I learned my lesson from personal experience, and I will embarrassingly share it with you here. Before this whole real estate investing game got really serious, I had become accustomed to filing my own taxes using TurboTax. When I got to 4 properties, I felt like the whole process was getting a bit overwhelming, so I found an accountant from a referral I received at work. I wasn't really sure at the time if I wanted to actually go through with paying for an accountant because I honestly didn't want to pay the $400 or so it was going to cost to have someone else file my paperwork. I was mainly going to seek some advice and see what he had to say, so I turned over all my information about every property and my previous tax returns and waited to hear back. Sure as shit the accountant came back to me and said... "Hey Art, I think you can do a lot better than what you have previously filed for deprecation." See at the time I wasn't as wise as I am now about all the write offs listed above so I wasn't 100% clear on what I was doing, even though I felt like an expert handling my own tax returns. After some more back and forth with the accountant, we ended up amending my previous years return to change up the deprecation and I ended up getting back an additional refund of around $4,000 from my previous years return. I was over here worried about spending $400 to have an expert in their field file my taxes, and I ended up getting back 10x that amount because the work was done properly.

This taught me a very important lesson that goes beyond doing your taxes.

> **Chapter Summary:**
> - Deprecation is one of the biggest tax write offs a rental property has during tax season.
> - There are specific reasons why the government allows for these big tax write offs and makes them available to real estate investors. Helping provide good housing for individuals looking to rent/buy and boosting the economy with big loans is a big deal.
> - You do not want to be living in conditions where the government is providing housing.

Chapter 13

Run It Like a Business, Man.

"Courage taught me no matter how bad a crisis gets.... Any sound investment will eventually pay off."

Carlos Slim Helu

I don't care if you have 1 small rental property that cost you $50,000 to purchase in the middle of nowhere or if you have 5 properties in expensive metro cities - no matter what your situation is you need to run your rental properties like a business. This doesn't mean go out and pay 10% of your rental income to a property manager and hope they do a good job because as I mentioned before, I am against hiring a property manager when you are still growing because it eats away at your cash flow, stunts your education on the process, and chances are the property manager won't care about your hard-earned equity as much as you will.

When I say you need to run it like a business, I mean you have to allow people who are experts in their field to do whatever work is necessary just like I learned to do with my accountant. If the gutters need to be cleaned, don't take your ladder to climb the roof and clean the gutters yourself. It's okay to spend the extra $150 or whatever it's going to cost you to hire a gutter cleaning service to come and do the job for you. There are 2 big reasons on why it is critical for you to run your rental properties like a business.

The first reason is it will force you to run your numbers more accurately when you're looking to make a purchase. When most people are trying to purchase a rental property and determining whether or not something is a good deal, a lot of times they will manipulate the numbers till they get the answer they want. This is especially true if you find a property that you really like. Someone who has the experience to repair small jobs here and there might not take into account the cost of labor to repair something at the property because they figure they can just take care of it themselves. As a result, they settle for a property where the profit isn't as high as it should be because they're assuming they will be doing most of the work. This isn't the game plan you want. You need to run your numbers considering the random miscellaneous things that inevitably are going to come up. I will give you a perfect example of something as recent as 2 weeks ago. The most recent duplex I purchased in Portland has quite a bit of large tree's all around the property and with large tree's come a lot of leaves. This causes the gutters to get filled up more often than I would like and it's something that needs to be addressed to keep your tenants happy! The thing is I knew this when I was purchasing the property, and I sure as hell knew I wasn't going to be climbing my ass up a ladder every few months to get these gutters cleaned. So every few months or so I know that I have to spend around $150-$200 to hire a professional company to come out to the property and get this done. If I was someone who thought I would be able to take on this cost and do the work myself I would have been content accepting an offer where my profit was less, because I wouldn't be taking this additional hit. This is what we want to avoid. Instead, I waited for a deal that made sense, while including these types of expenses, so now when I do have to pay for them I'm not breaking even that month with my cash flow or even worse going negative and having to pay out of my own pocket. Run your numbers the right way and include the monthly expenses you're going to have running a rental property business and you'll be better for it.

The second reason is so that you don't end up hating real estate investing. Honestly, whether you are a handyman or not, who the hell wants to clean gutters, pump toilets, and do all these nasty things when you can outsource it to someone who is a professional and knows what they're doing in that field. If you have to pick up phone calls about toilets and then go and do the work yourself, it's only a matter of time before you call it quits and end up hating the whole real estate game. You might even trick yourself and say you like doing these things to justify it, but the truth is it doesn't matter – You need to outsource repairs. Period. Do something more valuable with your time that's going to take you to the next level, instead of worrying about fixing miscellaneous crap at your property.

Run your property like a business and be the CEO. You need to be worried about profit & loss statements and tracking your balance sheet to see what you should be doing to increase your wealth – not cleaning gutters. This is the mindset difference between a business owner and a business employee. You can't be the employee in your own business. It's a different mindset and one that you need to be comfortable with to grow your business into an empire.

Chapter Summary:
- You need to treat your investments like a business. Doesn't matter if you have 1 small property or 20.
- Treating it like a business requires you to review financial statements, file your taxes properly, and most important of all make sure you are profitable!

Chapter 14

Anti-401K

"The biggest risk of all is not taking one."

Mellody Hobson

Do you know when you're investing into your 401K you pretty much have to estimate about what age you plan to die? If you retire with "X" amount of money in your 401K and you spend "X" amount per year, you will then have "X" number of years to enjoy that retirement money. Well shit, God forbid I live an extra 5 years more than I expected to, right? Its freaking hilarious, but at the same time depressing as hell. Does this sound like a solid plan to you? If you answered yes, please burn this book immediately.

"If you invest just $20 dollars a week, by the time you're 65 years old you will be a millionaire!" How many times have you heard or seen this bullshit being preached repeatedly by financial advisors all around to every single w2 employee they can find? They bust out their huge calculators to show you their version of "compound interest" to prove how much money you'll be making if you just keep investing with them you're entire life. Listen, if someone tells you to invest for

40+ years so you can retire a millionaire you better turn around and run in the completely opposite direction. Absolutely no one out there got rich following this process. All the rich people you see who invest in the market are already rich and made most of their money doing something else. Yes, if you're already rich and need a safe place to put your money and live off the interest then that's great, but financial freedom is not achieved by putting a small percentage in a 401k for multiple decades. The people who follow this plan are unfortunately individuals who just don't know any better. They see it as a safe way to invest because they don't want to take the time to educate themselves on money matters and would rather just put their entire future in the hands of some stranger. Most people follow this route so I'm sure we all know someone who thinks this is the right way to plan for retirement, but in today's world there is absolutely no excuse with the amount of free education that exists online. You just can't be naïve. While there is free education to be had, there are also hundreds of salesmen who are out there trying to sell you a dream just to take you on as a client. Know who to trust and know when you see the red flags, but the only way to identify either one of those things is to make sure you've educated yourself.

You don't need to abandon having a 401k altogether – Some corporations offer pretty good benefits when it comes to 401k accounts, and they'll match the amount you deposit up to a certain percentage which is a great resource you should take advantage of if you're able to. However, this should not be your primary plan for how you are building your wealth for the future. Some 401k accounts will even allow you to take a loan out and use the money for other investments, and I 100% am all about utilizing this tool if you know what you're doing. This gives you more control of your money rather than having it sit there and collect dust over 40 years. But again, you need to educate yourself – This doesn't mean take a loan out against your 401k and go buy yourself a nice car. It means take the money and find an appreciating asset that also gives you monthly cash flow, tax benefits, and loan pay down that increases your net worth every single month. Hmmm, I wonder what type of investment offers such amazing benefits... oh that's right, REAL ESTATE!

Skeptics will read this and say things like you know stuff like this isn't for everyone... Some people are just content with slowly and safely saving in a 401k account. Or they just don't have the knowledge or care to learn about any of this. After shedding a few tears, I would recommend they do some more research because at the end of the day, you're not going to fully understand the risk you're taking by not acting and putting your finances into your own hands till you're actually 65 years old and retiring. Only at that point will you look at your finances and say, oh no I only have enough money to live comfortably for about 10 years. Do you want to spend your entire life living frugally and saving for retirement, only to spend your retirement living more frugally just so you can guarantee yourself enough money till it's over? Or are you going to pray and depend on the government taking care of you with social security. This isn't the golden years you want believe me.

If you don't do it for yourself, do it for your parents because guess what? The above description is going to be the exact scenario your parents find themselves in much earlier than you will and they are going to depend on you to take care of them. Wouldn't it feel incredible to have this asset which you have all the control over, paying you every month with money that could be used to take care of your parents while also appreciating over the years? And the best part is this asset isn't something that's just going to disappear in 10 years. It's going to be around paying you till the end of time for generations and generations to come. It's pretty much like creating a never-ending flow of money – Who is in their right mind would not want this or would not create a few extra minutes during their day to educate themselves on it instead of scrolling through their phones on tik tok?

Do your homework. Learn how your money can best work for you instead of following what every corporate stooge does. Don't follow or believe the myth that a 401k is your path to financial freedom just because that's what 99% of the people out there do. You just need to take the initiative and grab control of your finances. This isn't something you want to do – It's something you NEED to do and that right there is the mindset difference between people who will achieve financial freedom and those who will not.

Chapter Summary:
- Do NOT associate retirement and financial freedom with old age.
- 401K's are not a bad thing if you understand what you're doing and if you're getting the best return possible with your money.
- With the amount of free information we have available online, there is no reason why anyone shouldn't understand how money works.
- If someone doesn't make understanding their financial situation a priority, then they are essentially saying they are okay with working their entire life with their retirement plans in the hands of someone they don't even know.

Chapter 15

Budgeting 101

"Know what you own and know why you own it."

Peter Lynch

A couple meet in college and go to medical school together cheering each other on for 7-10 years. They graduate and they feel powerful because they can now officially be called doctors. They go into the real world and get extremely high paying positions and are proud that all those years of school have officially paid off. Sounds like a fairy tale ending, doesn't it? This couple should be set for the rest of their life. But then the devil enters the equation...

They're doctors and getting paid well – So obviously they need to go out and buy the nicest home they can find and after they buy the home, they obviously both need super fancy cars to park in the driveway. But it doesn't end there, because now they need fancy furniture to place inside of their fancy house, and obviously they also need to take exquisite vacations a few times a year to show how well they're doing in life – They are well paid doctors after all... And before you know it, this couple who spent 10 years going to school in order to get great paying jobs are scratching and clawing their way through life because of all the materialistic crap out there.

This is not a knock-on school. We can save a whole other chapter for that. This is a knock on how people don't know how to budget or for those who just care more about their appearance. I painted a pretty extreme scenario, but the truth is this same idea applies to people in all different walks of life, whether they are a doctor or a schoolteacher. I don't care if you're getting paid 200k a year or 50k a year. Wealth is not measured by your income, its measured by your net worth.

I don't know who needs to hear this but it's OKAY if you don't have the newest Mercedes to drive. It's OKAY if you don't have a 5 thousand square foot house. No one cares. And if they care, they're probably not the people you should have in your life. This doesn't mean we shouldn't be striving to have those things... it means we shouldn't be jeopardizing our future net worth for it. There are many people out there who make a lot more money than I do from my w2 job. But I can confidently say my net worth is probably higher than 90% of those people who are making more annually at their profession. As good as it might feel to have all the nice toys in the present, you are essentially screwing over your future self.

I would take the schoolteacher on my team any day who is making 50k a year but living off of 40k and using the additional 10k as a down payment to buy a real estate asset over the doctor who is making 200k a year but spending 220k a year to have the nice car, the nice boat, the fancy house but is secretly living off of credit. That schoolteacher making 50k a year is going to have 10 properties in 10 years and is not going to need a job anymore for the rest of their life because they're going to be too busy collecting their monthly rent, while the doctor is still slaving away at their job every single day just to keep up their appearance.

All this leads back to financial literacy. You need to understand how money works and how you can put your own money to work for you. The more your money works for you, the less you will have to work. Stop caring about what others think and stop following the latest trend you see on Instagram because when you have a mountain of debt piled up and don't know what to do, none of those individuals are going to be there to feed you.

When you were growing up and in grade school, your report card was how everyone rated your performance. As an adult, most people think your credit report is how you're graded. Your credit report is very important yes, but many poor people can have good credit. This doesn't mean they have a solid understanding of money. It just means they pay their bills on time. The real way to grade your adult report card is through your income statement and your balance sheet. If you don't know what your current income statement and balance sheet look like for your personal finances, then I challenge you to take a deeper look at where your money is going.

Income Statement

Income
What the middle class focus on   W2 Job   Small Business
Expenses

Balance Sheet

Assets	Liabilities
What the wealthy focus on	*What the middle class waste their money on*
Real Estate	Cars
Stocks	Credit Cards
Big Business	

Where is most of your cash coming from? Where is most of your cash going? The wealthy focus on their assets, and turn their assets into income, whereas the poor and middle class don't have any assets at all and only care about getting a 3% raise at their w2 job.

Your car is not an asset. Your 15K credit line is not an asset. Your purses, shoes, suits, dresses are not assets. Assets generate income. If you placed something in the "Assets" box on your balance sheet, but there is no money being generated by the asset and flowing into your "income" box, then it is not an asset. Even if something is appreciating over time, but not providing you monthly income now, you can't classify that as an asset. Markets fluctuate and change all the time and if the gain isn't being realized then it is not an asset.

Proper budgeting requires financial knowledge. The way to escape the middle class and create real wealth for your family is to have cash flowing assets be your main source of income. Shift your focus to how you can add more in the assets box, rather than focusing on how to get pocket-sized raises in your income box. If you master this while also limiting the number of items you have in your liabilities box, you are guaranteed to escape the middle class and achieve financial freedom at an early age. It's not easy. Especially as you look around and see everyone flaunting their materialistic crap on social media, but at the end of the day you have to ask yourself how badly do you want it?

Chapter Summary:
- Do not make poor financial decisions to impress others, or because you crave instant gratification.
- Learn how money works, and how you can use it to achieve financial independence. All this starts with budgeting, and it doesn't matter how much money you make.
- Know the difference between an asset and a liability. Is most of your income being generated by assets or from a w2 job?

Chapter 16

Appreciate the Appreciation

"Investing should be more like watching paint dry or watching grass grow. If you want excitement, take $800 and go the Las Vegas."

Paul Samuelson

During the 2007-2008 housing crisis I was still a child sucking on my thumbs so I'm not going to sit here and pretend like I know everything that went down during that time, but I've read quite a few books and educated myself. This was important for me to do and I recommend everyone who is interested in getting into real estate do the same. This specific time frame is what scared many people away from real estate and has left them scarred till this day.

There are 2 things that stood out to me and we've covered both of them in previous chapters. Over-leverage and cash flow (running your numbers properly) – These two pretty much go hand in hand and is what caused investors and home buyers to lose their homes during this time.

Everyone and anyone was getting approved for a loan whether they were actually able to afford it or not while keeping their fingers crossed hoping the property would keep appreciating. In a way I feel extremely fortunate I jumped into the real estate game on the backend of the housing crises, so I didn't feel this take place first-hand and have had the fortune of buying rentals with values on an upward climb. Having said that, it doesn't mean I'm going to go out there and make stupid decisions with my money because I know better whether I lived through the housing crises or not.

During this time home appreciation was taken for granted – People did not appreciate the appreciation. This is something that takes time to learn, and I'll admit when I was first getting started I didn't realize how important of a rule this was which everyone needed to follow. Usually when someone is first getting started in real estate and they're just trying to get their foot through the door, they will take the most horrible financing options just to close on the purchase. Yes, it's true that banks nowadays are much stricter on financing and shouldn't be approving loans unless they are sure it can be paid back, but that doesn't mean you should go out there and get an FHA loan for 3.5% on a $700,000 property and pay a ridiculous amount every single month. If you're someone who lives in an expensive market, this is not an uncommon scenario I just described. This is how you get yourself in trouble. This applies to both an investor and a regular home buyer.

For starters, you are over-leveraged on this loan right out the gate. If you were to turn around and sell this home 2 weeks later, you would lose money after you account for your fees and agent commissions. You have put yourself at the mercy of appreciation because there is absolutely no way you're going to pay down this loan to a reasonable equity position anytime in the next 7-10 years. You are hoping your home appreciates otherwise if there is any type of market correction you will be upside down on the loan and still stuck with an astronomical mortgage payment every single month. If you are willing to put yourself in this situation you better have a big cash of reserves saved up in your bank account to make sure you're protecting yourself if anything goes wrong. Otherwise, if you do this AND you have no reserves as a back-up plan you are literally praying to whoever your God is every night hoping nothing goes wrong. This isn't the kind of stress you want to add to your life when you're buying a property.

All this said leads directly to cash flow and whether or not you ran your numbers correctly. There are states and cities specifically in the mid-west where you can take out a loan and be extremely over-leveraged, but still produce cash flow every month from the rents you're collecting because the properties are so cheap. If you've ran your numbers well and you're producing great profit month over month with rents, then you can make up for the horrible financing this way and

I am all for it. The reason why this is okay is because even if there is a market correction, or something unexpected does happen, your monthly rent still covers everything for you. You just better make sure your tenant screening is great because it makes having a good tenant that pays on time every month more critical in this situation.

However, if you live in an expensive market where you took out a horrible loan AND you aren't producing any decent monthly income from your rents, I have no sympathy for you and I almost hope you learn your lesson the hard way. You cannot buy a property just so you can say you bought a property. This is like the blind leading the blind. You're just speculating and hoping for appreciation. Don't be this person. Don't take appreciation for granted. When you're buying a property make sure you run the numbers and it makes sense, even if the bank is willing to give you a loan without doing so. This is what makes you a true investor – Investors spend more time saying no to deals than actually purchasing them because they have a very picky selection process and aren't going to put their money at risk to buy a property just because. So have an investor mindset, run your numbers, and only follow through if all the boxes have been checked whether you're an investor or a first-time home buyer.

Chapter Summary:
- We need to learn from the past and the past tells us that when people buy investment properties for the sole purpose of making money on appreciation, the odds are they will not be successful.
- Take advantage of the appreciation in your properties, but do not buy a property that is going to lose you money every single month and do not create this scenario by doing a cash out refinance on a property either.

Chapter 17

DTI

"Wide diversification is only required when investors do not understand what they are doing."

Warren Buffett

No, DTI does not stand for down to invest even though I personally feel like that would be a better use of the acronym. DTI stands for Debt-to-Income ratio and its one of the important numbers your lenders going to be looking at when you're trying to get approved for a loan so it's important that you know exactly where you stand with your financial ratio. It's a very simple calculation and there are hundreds of calculators you can find online that will help you break this down. You essentially need to add up all the monthly payments that you've promised to pay to others. This includes but is not limited to your credit card minimum payments, any car loans or leases to your name, student loans, etc. You do not need to count things like utilities or a cell phone bill. After you have your debt total, add up your pre-tax gross income.

Once you have those two numbers you take the total debt and divide it by the total gross income.

Anything below 35% is considered really strong and you will have no issues getting approved for the loan, assuming you make enough money to pay for the new mortgage. You're able to get pre-approved as long as you fall below the 50% mark on a conventional loan, but the closer you get to 50% the more challenging it becomes. and the more questions get asked by the underwriter. A perfect example of how I experienced this personally was a couple years ago when I was trying to get a loan approved for a cash-out refinance on one of my properties in California. I was on the brink of that 50% debt-to-income ratio percentage so the underwriter was giving me all sorts of crap. I had 2 credit cards with balances. One card had a $125 balance, and the other had a $40 balance. Each card had a minimum $25 payment a month. The underwriter literally made one of the terms of the approval be me paying these cards off in full with the cash-out refinance payout. Mind you the cash-out was around $105,000. No, these numbers are not typos. We're REALLY talking about a total balance of $165 between two credit cards with $25 minimum payments. I honestly have been through a bunch of crap in the past trying to get loans approved, but this one just got under my skin – at the end of the day all I could do was laugh about it and say yes sure, I'll pay off my $165 dollars in credit card debt for you. Absolutely ridiculous.

One of the reasons why I've grown fond of purchasing 2-unit duplexes is actually because they are much easier to qualify for than a single-family home. When you're purchasing a duplex as a primary residence, meaning you're going to live on one side and rent the other side to a tenant, you get to count the rent as part of your qualification process for the loan. So, if you purchase a duplex and your all-in monthly upkeep of the loan is $2,000 a month, but you can rent one side of the duplex for $1,000 a month, then you really only have to qualify for half the amount. You can almost say it's a cheat code to getting approved for a mortgage loan.

At the end of the day, when you're deciding to jump into the game and purchase a property the less surprises you have the better because there's already going to be enough things that stress you out throughout the process. So have an idea of what your DTI ratio is when you first start the process, and if the percentage isn't what you need it to be, then start planning on what you can change now instead of putting it off and having it be the reason you never get started.

Debt-to-Income Ratio

- DTI IS THE PERCENTAGE LENDERS USE TO SEE WHAT LOAN AMOUNT YOU QUALIFY FOR ON A MORTGAGE.
- YOU SIMPLY ADD UP ALL YOUR MONTHLY DEBT PAYMENTS AND DIVIDE IT BY YOUR MONTHLY GROSS INCOME.

PAYMENTS TO INCLUDE:
- RENT / MORTGAGE
- AUTO LOAN PAYMENT
- STUDENT LOAN PAYMENT
- CREDIT CARD MINIMUM PAYMENT
- PERSONAL LOAN PAYMENT

PAYMENTS TO NOT INCLUDE:
- CELL PHONE PAYMENT
- HOME UTILITY PAYMENTS
- INSURANCE PREMIUMS

EXAMPLE:

EXPENSES

MORTGAGE: 1,000
CREDIT CARD PAYMENT: $200
AUTO LOAN PAYMENT: $400

INCOME

PRE-TAX GROSS INCOME: $3,500

$1,600 ÷ $3,500 = DTI 45%

- You will need a DTI less than 50% to qualify for a conventional loan.
- Anything 35% or lower is considered really strong.

Chapter Summary:
- It's important for you to have an idea of what your DTI is before applying for a loan.
- Once you have a better idea, you can take specific actions to improve the overall percentage. Utilize the thousands of free calculators you can find online.

Chapter 18

Inspection Period Is Your Best Friend

> *"A lot of people with high IQs are terrible investors because they've got terrible temperaments. You need to keep raw, irrational emotion under control."*
>
> *Charlie Munger*

Imagine being able to pick the best car of your choosing, driving it off the lot and take it for a joy ride for 2 weeks, while testing every inch of the ride. Then and ONLY then, if you like what you saw, you make your decision to go through with it and officially purchase the vehicle. That's kind of what the home inspection period does for you when you're purchasing a new property!

Let's get one thing straight – Seller's hate inspection periods and the longer the inspection period is on your original offer, the less chances of you getting your offer accepted. The reason why most seller's hate the inspection period is because most of the time after the inspection is completed, buyers will try and negotiate the price, or even the repairs they want the seller to complete before closing. This puts many sellers in a bad position because at this point they are locked into the deal and if they decide they want to hold firm and not concede anything, they risk the potential of losing the deal. There are 2 main reasons why this could be bad for the seller. For starters, the seller has already been locked into the deal for around 2 weeks at this point. That's 2 weeks of lost days if the buyer decides to back out. Homes in escrow take 30-45 days to close and re starting that process with a new buyer would take additional time and potentially more payments the seller needs to make to their mortgage lender during that time. Trust me, when you're in contract and trying to sell your home, the last thing you want to worry about is having to make another expensive payment to your lender for your own mortgage loan. The seller's lender doesn't care that the house is getting sold soon, they just care about getting their payment on time. And plus, that money from the sale might be needed as soon as possible so any additional day could be costly.

The second reason this puts sellers in a bad position if the deal were to fall apart, is it makes the property look like something might be wrong with it to the rest of the world when the listing goes back on the market. Think about it... If a home you were interested in buying were to get an accepted offer by someone else, and two weeks later the home was back on the market wouldn't you be questioning why? Something might be wrong with the home... why else would the original buyer back out? This results in many people becoming hesitant which in turn will hurt the value of the home. Offers after that might not be as high because potential buyers now smell blood in the water, and they know the seller is in a bad spot. For an investor this creates opportunity. Knowing this information gives us the opportunity to make an offer a little less than what we originally would have had to put, and it makes the seller more likely to accept!

Now that we have an idea of what the inspection period is like from the seller's point of view, lets shift gears and discuss why the inspection period is the buyer's best friend for reasons in addition to what we already mentioned above.

In a sellers' market, which we're in right now in 2021, its very challenging to get an offer accepted because every listing seems to get into a multiple offer situation. One way to make your offer more enticing to the seller without waiving your inspection contingency is to put a large earnest money deposit. The earnest money deposit is usually around 1-2% of the home purchase price, and it's the first deposit the buyer must make to the escrow company when an offer is accepted when you're financing the home. Knowing most people put 1-2% deposit on their earnest money, it's wise to stand out and put 2-5% instead. A large earnest deposit makes you appear like a serious buyer who really wants to purchase the home. It also shows you have strong buying power since you're willing to forgo such a large amount just for the earnest money. Most people fear doing this because if the contract were to fall apart during escrow due to the buyer not being able to close, then they forfeit their earnest money to the seller. You can kind of think about earnest money as the collateral for the seller in case something were to go wrong with the deal. The thing is this is very rare. The buyer has so many opportunities to walk away from the deal without losing their earnest money, it's not something that should scare you from putting a large earnest deposit. And this is what leads us to why the inspection period is so critical.

The typical number of days included for the inspection period in a purchase agreement contract is 8 business days. During this time the buyer will usually pay for a professional inspection and they will receive a very thorough report regarding everything about the property. If there are specific things you want the inspector to focus on, then you're able to talk through all those points with whoever you are hiring to do the job. Once you receive this report, you have the option to go back to the seller and ask them to repair certain line items, ask them to lower the selling price because of certain things you discovered after the inspection, or choose simply to proceed without asking the seller to concede anything. During this 8-day window you have the opportunity to walk away from the deal if you don't feel comfortable moving forward. If you decide the property isn't for you and you walk away, you do not lose your earnest money and it will get refunded back to you. Therefore, putting in a large earnest deposit is not something to shy away from, especially if you know it will make your offer stand out!

I will add that during this hot seller's market, more and more buyers are waiving their inspection contingency to make their offer more enticing to the seller. If you are an experienced buyer and know what to look for in a house when it comes to potential expensive repairs, then this might be okay for you to do. However, if you are just starting out and need the expertise of someone else when it comes to the condition of the property, I do not advise you to waive your inspection contingency. If you do and discover something wrong with the property that makes you want to walk away, you still can, however you will need to surrender your earnest money to the seller. In some cases that might still be okay because I rather lose my earnest money than worry about purchasing a property that may need thousands more in repairs, but again this is not something I would advise for someone who is just getting started.

Chapter Summary:
- Treat the inspection period for your purchase similar to how you would treat a test drive for a new car.
- You can make your offer more enticing with a large earnest deposit knowing you can back out anytime during the inspection period.
- If you are someone who does not know what to look for when walking a property, do not skip on the inspection contingency, even if it does make your offer less attractive.
- Sellers hate the inspection contingency

Chapter 19

Pre-Approval

"The four most dangerous words in investing are: 'this time it's different.' "

Sir John Templeton

We talked a little about the documents you need for the beginning of your loan process earlier in the book, but I want to dive into why the pre-approval step is such a big one when you're starting the process of looking for a property.

If you're someone who is just starting out, or even someone who has quite a few properties already but is only buying 1-2 homes a year, you're likely not someone who is talking to lenders, agents, and everyone else who would be a part of your real estate journey on a consistent basis. When you're not talking to these individuals on a consistent basis and purchasing multiple homes throughout the year, the chances of them taking you seriously without a pre-approval is not likely. Especially in today's 2021 market, agents have so many clients looking to purchase a new home and they already have a lot on their plate, so if you approach them with the mindset of "yeah I'm interested in real estate, and

I'm looking to jump in but I'm not really sure exactly what I'm looking for just yet" there is no way the agent is going to prioritize you. Why would they? Agents do not make an hourly wage so they aren't getting paid for the time they spend talking to your ass so why would they take up their valuable time if you aren't someone who is prepared? Always put yourself in the other persons shoes and view things from their perspective before getting upset as to why this individual isn't treating you like royalty just because you told them you're interested in buying a property.

However, if you were someone who was prepared and took the time to get your ducks in a row and had your pre-approval ready, THEN you went to the agent and said "hey, I have my pre-approval ready, and I'm looking in this specific area for a 3-bedroom home in this price range" now we're talking. That agent is going to listen to every word you tell them, and best believe when something within those parameters comes up on their list, you are going to be the first person they call. This makes the agent want to work with you. This makes the agent take you seriously. And the only difference between the 2 scenarios is you having your pre-approval ready and knowing exactly what you're shopping for.

The same applies when you're talking to lenders. Most people shop different lenders to get the best possible interest rate they can, and even though this isn't something

I'm necessarily against doing, it does open the door for the lender not to take you seriously once again. Lenders know you're shopping around, and they don't want their time wasted either. So what I would rather do when it comes to the lender is go to someone that I know is good at what they do based on referrals or previous personal experiences and let them know that you want to work with them. Let them know exactly what you're looking for, and get your pre-approval done. This type of commitment makes the loan officer, lender want to work hard for you because of the trust you've put in them. Obviously, there will be exceptions here, but if they are someone who is good at their job, this will only make life easier and the better the relationship with your lender, the less headaches you're going to have to go through during the loan process.

So, it's that simple. If you want to be taken seriously get your pre-approval done. Once its complete, your pre-approval is usually good for 4 months, so it's not like you have to buy a place right away. You can still take your time, and even if you don't find a place or change your mind it's not the end of the world, but at least you know you're prepared and ready in case something you like comes up!

Chapter Summary:
- You need to know what you qualify for before beginning your search. Otherwise, you're just wasting everyone's time.
- Just because you have enough saved money in your bank account, it does not mean the lender will qualify you for a mortgage.

Chapter 20

Property Classes

"An investment in knowledge pays the best interest."

Benjamin Franklin

If you want to get started in real estate investing, you need to understand the different types of property classes that exist. If you don't understand the different types of classes, how are you supposed to know what type of property you're looking to buy?

I came across this saying recently and it perfectly sums up the importance of property classes. The saying goes "Desirable properties attract desirable tenants. Disgusting properties attract disgusting tenants." Now I know this might be a little harsh, but there is a lot of truth in this. Earlier in the book we talked about why some places around the country, specifically in the Midwest, have such low home values. Well, those locations more than likely are not Class A locations, and therefore they aren't going to attract a premium rent or a premium tenant and that is extremely important when looking to buy a rental property. This doesn't mean you have to always be buying the best of the best — in most cases this shouldn't even be your #1 option because in most Class A properties there isn't enough cash flow month to month because of the premium price you're paying for the property. Take a second to view the table below. This gives you a great look into what categorizes the different classes in real estate.

REAL ESTATE PROPERTY CLASSES

Tycoon Realty Holdings

	Class A	Class B	Class C	Class D
PROPERTY TYPE:	NEWER, RECENTLY BUILT W/ LUXURY FINISHES.	LESS THAN 20 YEARS OLD, AVERAGE FINISHES.	20+ YEARS OLD, MAINTENANCE AND REPAIR COSTS WILL BE HIGHER.	50+ YEARS OLD, VACANT, BOARDED UP PROPERTIES
AFFORDABILITY:	PRICED ON THE HIGHER END. LOW CASH FLOW POTENTIAL	LOW VACANCY RATES, HIGH RENTS	MID-LOW RANGE, GOOD CASH FLOW ON PAPER.	VERY AFFORDABLE, HIGH COST OF REPAIRS.
LIVABILITY:	LOW CRIME RATES, MORE OWNER-OCCUPIED OWNERS.	LOW CRIME RATES, OWNER-OCCUPIED STILL OVERWEIGHS RENTALS	HIGHER CRIME RATE, TYPICALLY NON-VIOLENT. MORE RENTAL PROPERTIES	HIGH CRIME RATE, RENTERS OUTWEIGH HOMEOWNERS
AMENITIES:	GREAT NEARBY AMENITIES, PARKS, MALLS, ETC.	GOOD AMENITIES, JOBS, SCHOOLS ARE NEARBY.	AMENITIES ARE NOT NEARBY.	ALMOST NO ACCESS TO GOOD AMENITIES, JOBS OR SCHOOLS

- INVESTORS WILL UTILIZE THESE CATEGORIES WHEN ANALYZING DIFFERENT MARKETS.
- IT IS NOT UNCOMMON TO HEAR AN INVESTOR SAY THEY ARE LOOKING IN A CLASS B NEIGHBORHOOD FOR A CLASS C PROPERTY - THIS OFFERS THE POTENTIAL FOR IMMEDIATE EQUITY AFTER SOME MINOR REPAIRS

As you can see in the diagram, property age, vacancy rates, own/rent ratio, crime rates, nearby amenities, and many other factors are used when evaluating a property class. The most ideal properties for investment purposes really sit between the B and C section. This is where you get the most bang for your buck. Here is a perfect example of what I'm usually looking for when shopping for a new rental.

I want a class C property but in a class B neighborhood and here is why. Class B neighborhood puts me where I want to be because I still get the low vacancy rates and high rents that the class A would offer, but without the premium price since the properties aren't brand new. In addition to the class B neighborhood, I would want a class C property because this will give me the discount I'm looking for in terms of home price. Class C properties usually need some cosmetic work and are usually priced below market value

You should know the area you're looking to invest in like the back of your hand. Cities always have good and bad pockets, and one block can look/feel drastically different than the one next to it. If you have truly done your homework and have a good understanding of the location you are trying to invest in, then you should be able to tell within a few seconds what property class a specific property falls under. Only then should you be 100% confident that you've done the proper research!

Chapter Summary:
- It's important to know exactly what type of property you're looking to invest in when making the decision to purchase an investment property.
- Being able to easily identify these different types of property characteristics is one of the ways you become great at spotting potentially good deals.

Chapter 21

Tenant Screening

"When you invest, you are buying a day that you don't have to work."

Aya Laraya

Would you allow just anyone into your inner circle? Would you share your most personal thoughts with just any stranger? I would like to assume you wouldn't. So why would you rent your property which you worked so hard to purchase, with your hard-earned money to someone without doing the proper research? This doesn't mean you need to be close friends with your tenants or have it be someone you personally know. I would actually advise against this because you don't want to mix your business with your personal relationships, but this doesn't mean you allow just anyone to live at your property.

There are many platforms you can use when you're finally ready to screen a tenant and I talked about how I personally utilize the Zillow platform earlier in the book. That being said, the platform you use really doesn't matter, but what you're looking for in the actual screening is what counts.

Before ever looking at an application, you should already have outlined the pre-requisites you're looking for in a potential tenant. You need to take this step seriously because one bad tenant can ruin your entire investment. You are the one on the hook with the lender, not your tenant so the bank is coming after you if they are not paid. The Covid-19 lockdown was a great example of how unforeseen circumstances can really hurt you if you're not careful. No one can predict something like that ever happening, but what you can do is be very meticulous with your screening process and make sure you're only putting in tenants that meet your criteria, who would be more likely to be able to get through an economic slowdown like the one we experienced during Covid-19. For example, individuals who have a great credit score are more likely to care about their financial situation and take it more seriously because they don't want their credit score to be impacted by an eviction stain on their credit report.

So, what are the most critical guidelines to screening the best tenant? This could vary and be different depending on your location and circumstance, but I will share what I look for during my own process.

1. Credit score at or above 700

a. This might sound high, but it shouldn't be for someone who simply just pays their basic bills in a timely manner.

2. 1+ year with the same employer

a. Consistent time with a single employer speaks volumes on stability. You do not want someone who has a new career path every 6 months, or someone who is looking for new work every year. Could they potentially have moved on for a better opportunity? Yes, but most people don't jump from job to job every year. This is a red flag and could mean they aren't a reliable employee, and if they aren't a reliable employee, there is a higher risk they aren't going to be a reliable tenant either.

3. 1+ year living at prior addresses

a. The reasons behind this are very similar to what I just stated about 1+ year with the same employer. Most people don't move from place to place every year, and if its less than a year that's even a bigger red flag. Most people sign a year long lease at the beginning, and if there stay was for 6 months at their previous address chances are they broke that lease with the previous landlord. Again, this could be due to unforeseen circumstances like a relationship gone bad, or work relocation, but these are the types of things you need to be on the lookout for when you're collecting your data.

4. Monthly income 2x asking rent

a. To be honest, 2x rent is on the low end of what most others would be looking for so this could be adjusted a bit if necessary. Financial advisors would tell you the amount you're paying for rent should not exceed 30% of the income you're bringing home. So, when you're looking at income vs. rent you also need to pay attention to what other liabilities the individual has on their credit report. If they have car loans, student loans, credit card payments, etc. that will eat up the remainder of what they have left over after they pay rent then that's your red flag. You do not want a tenant knowing they are going to be scrapping every last dollar every month to make their rent payment. You're not only doing this for yourself, but also for them. They should not be making that type of poor financial decision and instead be looking for a place that's a little easier on their wallet.

These are the four bullets I take into consideration with every potential tenant. The platform you use will give you background and credit reports which will give you this information. You just need to take the additional step and do the research. Research should not only consist of looking at the information but also making the call to the employer to make sure they are in good standing, and also call the previous addresses they have stayed at to see what the landlord has to say. Obviously take what the current landlord has to say with a grain of salt because they could just be trying to get rid of a bad tenant. That's why its good to go back to 2 previous landlords.

Doing all this might seem like a ton, but it really is only about an hour or 2 of your time which isn't much considering how important of a decision this is. So do the work and get yourself a good tenant. And if you're someone who doesn't do any of this and just puts the first person they see in as a tenant then I will be praying for you.

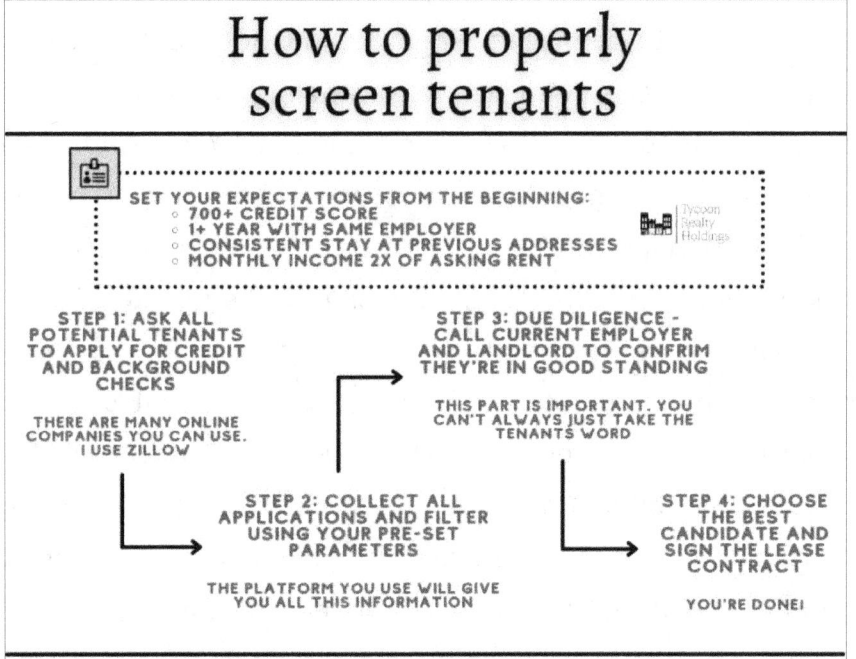

- It only takes one bad tenant to ruin your investment
- Take the time to do your research even if it takes a bit longer than expected to find a good candidate
- Couple months of no rent collected are better than rushing and getting stuck with a horrible tenant.

Chapter Summary:
- Screen your tenants and know what you're looking for in a tenant before even starting the process.
- Call current employers and previous landlords to confirm all the information.
- Do not place a tenant in your property without doing any of this research.

Chapter 22

Summary

"Winning makes you different, and different scares people"

— Tim Grover

I heard Tim Grover say this quote during a podcast and it just stuck with me.

Many like the ideology of investing in real estate, and even more enjoy talking about it - But how many people do you know who actually do it and do it successfully? After reading this book are you willing to study the MLS on a daily basis? Are you willing to go walk open houses every single weekend? Are you consistently going to pull up rent comparisons in your area to have a good understanding of what the rental market is like for the properties you're interested in?

Just because someone buys a piece of property it does not make them an investor, the same way everyone who makes it to the NBA isn't Kobe Bryant. Winning means putting in the work, and most people simply aren't willing to. You can spot people who aren't willing to put in the work when you start to hear comments like... " the market is too hot to buy anything right now" or "I'm just going to wait it out till the market crashes." The truth is if you're built to win and are willing to do what it takes, then there will always be opportunities for you. This is what separates the winners from the people who are just too scared to do anything. They're not scared of the end result, because let's face it, everyone wants the end result. They're scared of the work that's going to be required of them in order to reach that end result.

Chapter Summary:
- This isn't something you can half ass your way through. Jump in with both feet and dedicate your time. If you aren't willing to dedicate time to something that could allow you the freedom to do whatever you want with your time in the future, then your priorities in life need to be addressed first.

THANK YOU.

www.ingramcontent.com/pod-product-compliance
Lightning Source LLC
Chambersburg PA
CBHW071411210526
45465CB00001B/334